ADVANCES IN DEMOCRACY

FROM THE FRENCH REVOLUTION TO THE PRESENT-DAY EUROPEAN UNION

A History of Western Civilization

ADVANCES IN DEMOCRACY

FROM THE FRENCH REVOLUTION TO THE PRESENT-DAY EUROPEAN UNION

Edited by Heather M. Campbell, Senior Editor, Geography and History

Britannica Educational Publishing

in association with

ROSEN

EDUCATIONAL SERVICES

Published in 2011 by Britannica Educational Publishing
(a trademark of Encyclopædia Britannica, Inc.)
in association with Rosen Educational Services, LLC
29 East 21st Street, New York, NY 10010.

Distributed exclusively by Rosen Educational Services.
For a listing of additional Britannica Educational Publishing titles, call toll free (800) 237-9932.

First Edition

Britannica Educational Publishing
Michael I. Levy: Executive Editor
J.E. Luebering: Senior Manager
Marilyn L. Barton: Senior Coordinator, Production Control
Steven Bosco: Director, Editorial Technologies
Lisa S. Braucher: Senior Producer and Data Editor
Yvette Charboneau: Senior Copy Editor
Kathy Nakamura: Manager, Media Acquisition
Heather M. Campbell: Senior Editor, Geography and History

Rosen Educational Services
Shalini Saxena: Editor
Nelson Sá: Art Director
Cindy Reiman: Photography Manager
Matthew Cauli: Designer, Cover Design
Introduction by Joyce Nagle

Library of Congress Cataloging-in-Publication Data

Advances in democracy: from the French Revolution to the present-day European Union/ edited by Heather M. Campbell. — 1st ed.
p. cm. — (A history of Western civilization)
"In association with Britannica Educational Publishing, Rosen Educational Services."
Includes bibliographical references and index.
ISBN 978-1-61530-337-3 (library binding)
1. Europe—Civilization—18th century. 2. Europe—Civilization—19th century.
3. Europe—Civilization—20th century. 4. Civilization, Western.
5. Civilization, Modern—1950- 6. Democracy—Europe—History. I. Campbell, Heather M.
CB411.A38 2011
909'.09821—dc22

2010032147

Manufactured in the United States of America

On the cover: East German border guards stand along the top of the Berlin Wall facing a man waving the German national flag. Following the opening of the border between East and West Germany on November 9, 1989, the country was united under a single government and banner. *Tom Stoddart Archive/Edit/Getty Images*

On page x: Heroes of the French Revolution are depicted in a statue that stands in the Panthéon in Paris. *Shutterstock.com*

On pages 1, 40, 71, 93, 128, 150, 188, 218, 220, 222: Map of present-day Europe. *Courtesy of the University of Texas Libraries, The University of Texas at Austin*

CONTENTS

86

98

110

136

152

179

196

206

INTRODUCTION

Modern democracy, while rooted in the ancient civilizations of Greece and Rome, was propelled by the players, beliefs, and events of Europe in the 18th, 19th, and 20th centuries. Grounded by enlightened optimism about progress, liberty, and human rights, modern Europeans reinvented their political, economic, and social institutions to reflect these new ideals. Indeed, they waged battle for these beliefs through a series of revolutions that would transform daily life and expectations for every social class. Large-scale political and economic movements, like the French Revolution, combined with significant unintended consequences to spread democratic change throughout the continent. Driven largely by Great Britain and France, innovation and change started in the west and gradually moved eastward.

As democracy advanced, it transformed all aspects of European life largely because the improvements it brought were self-evident—even to the mass of people who did not initially profit from them. As each succeeding group recognized that it, too, stood to gain, democracy became an irresistible force. This volume examines modern Europe, from 1789, the start of the French Revolution, to the present day, and explains how democratic impulses in economics, politics, and philosophy combined to change the world.

Determining the rank and importance of a myriad of democratizing ideas and events is often complex because key events in Europe unfolded both gradually and simultaneously, each affecting the other. Nevertheless, several events stand out as formative to the democratic process. The first is the Industrial Revolution. Made possible by the agricultural revolution, which provided a stable and plentiful food supply, the Industrial Revolution transformed society through robust commercialization. Many profited, or hoped to profit, from increasing economic activity; attracted by the promise of steady employment, workers relocated to urban settings as villages swelled into industrial cities. With luck and grit, a family of hard workers could improve their standard of living and perhaps, to a limited extent, their class standing. Social mobility meant increased educational opportunities for children, and disposable income turned the worker into a consumer with new tastes and expectations.

Even the problems of urbanization spurred democratic thinking as municipal governments were forced to expand. The result of this expansion was a large professional bureaucracy that created systems and infrastructure to deal with crime, poverty, and public health. The growing power of these urban centres forced national governments, like that of Great Britain, to redistribute political power from rural to urban areas. Modern industrial society required an educated work force, and this, too, exacerbated expectations for social and economic mobility and commensurate political rights.

New methods of accruing wealth swelled the ranks of the bourgeoisie (middle class). As their wealth and educational achievements grew, members of the bourgeoisie expected a commensurate growth in political influence and power. Societies that lagged behind, notably in eastern and southern Europe, struggled to make the industrial transition and in that struggle were forced to extend at least limited rights to their lower classes. Everywhere pressure to change was accompanied by a reactionary pressure to exploit. This gave rise to riots, revolts, and revolutions in both the east and the west. The most spectacular and groundbreaking of these, the French Revolution, was the second formative event of the modern era.

The ideological basis for the French Revolution was the 18th-century intellectual movement known as the Enlightenment. This movement did more than spark a revolution, however: the Enlightenment is uniformly recognized as the philosophical key that opened the door to the modern world. Enlightenment thinkers shaped a worldview that was confident in the abilities of people to construct a more humane and rational society through new systems of representative government based on free speech, freer economic development, and religious tolerance.

The centre of the movement was in France, where the rising bourgeoisie and demoralized lower nobility were becoming increasingly frustrated by the autocratic and mercantilist policies of the divine-right Bourbon monarchy. The well-educated and overtaxed bourgeoisie became a willing audience for the subversive works of writers like Denis Diderot and Jean-Jacques Rousseau. Their ideas were intended to be democratizing in several important ways. First, they were often written for the ordinary man as a means to extend his education. They also elevated the occupations and contributions of the bourgeoisie and put the old regime on notice that new values, like meritocracy and freedom of thought, were replacing traditional ways. Innovation and progress, in service to the common good, became the new standard. Over time, despite attempts to embrace ideas of the Enlightenment, France's corrupt and inefficient absolute monarchy became increasingly unable and unwilling to adapt to the changes that threatened its supremacy.

France's old regime was vulnerable to attack on several fronts. Enlightenment thinkers both criticized the status quo and offered promising innovations that appealed to the large, prosperous, and capable Third Estate, members of which included France's urban middle class. France was a wealthy nation, but the treasury faced insolvency despite heavy taxation of the Third Estate. Forced by economic crisis to reform the taxation system, a series of changing finance ministers were unable to gain the trust or cooperation of the nobles, and King Louis XVI reluctantly called the centuries-old representative body, the Estates-General, into session. When procedural infighting broke out, Louis aligned himself with the Third Estate in an effort to shore up support for the monarchy. However, unintended consequences stymied the crown's plans—the Third Estate agitated for the end of feudal dues, and equality before the law was firmly established with the adoption of the Declaration of the Rights of Man and the Citizen.

The French Revolution became a struggle between the moderate supporters of constitutional monarchy and the more radical forces that supported a French republic. The ostensibly republican Jacobin party emerged victorious but instituted what was in effect a dictatorship, eager to stamp out every remnant of the old regime. The subsequent ruling elite, while less bloodthirsty, was also less effective at thwarting challenges to democratic reform. Into the power vacuum stepped the brilliant general Napoleon Bonaparte.

Napoleon's rise to power through a coup d'état and his relentless pursuit of empire and imperial succession for his heirs might seem incongruous with his devotion to Enlightenment ideals. However, Napoleon did, in word and deed, advance the cause of democratization in several ways. As the dashing, self-actualized, Romantic hero of the day, he exemplified the ideals of meritocracy, individual agency, and human liberty. After all, the old regime would never have placed this Corsican son of a lawyer on the French throne.

In a sense, Napoleon represented the new man. Through initiative and determination he made the most of his education and then exploited the new political and social order to his advantage. What he did for himself, he allowed for others. Despite conveniently placing his family members on thrones, Napoleon did extend the message of meritocracy wherever he went and did, indeed, promote many individuals on the basis of their talent and accomplishments. A soldier's soldier, he spoke to his men as citizens, not subjects, raising them up in their own esteem.

If we are cynical about Napoleon's mixed record, the vast majority of the Frenchmen of his day were not—Napoleon was supported by huge majorities in every plebiscite he held. Once and for all, he broke the back of hereditary privilege in France. He unified the nation through the standardization of law with his legal code. He promoted secondary education by establishing lycées, secondary schools primarily for the children of the middle class. In addition, Napoleon managed to export enlightened thought in the countries he conquered. When speaking to the peoples of these nations, he spoke the language of Romantic nationalism, anthropomorphizing the nation with the positive attributes of the indigenous people. Napoleon's rhetoric gave voice to nationalistic yearnings throughout western Europe. Moreover, even the Congress of Vienna—the assembly called to reorganize European boundaries after the Napoleonic Wars—was not unmoved by the democratic sentiments sweeping the continent. However, after the defeat of Napoleon, "legitimate monarchs" were returned to their thrones with a warning from

Klemens, prince von Metternich, the principal minister of Austria, concerning the perils of autocratic rule in an enlightened age.

The ongoing battle for democratic advancement continued throughout the 19th century. Fueled by both Romantic nationalism and liberal aspirations, revolutions occurred throughout Europe. Greece enlisted the help of liberal admirers from across Europe in its war for independence from the Ottoman Empire, and volunteers like the English Romantic poet Lord Byron answered the call to arms, inspired by the thought of liberating the first democracy of the ancient world. Roman Catholic Belgium waged a successful war of independence from the Netherlands and adopted a bicameral parliamentary system. The unification of Italy made good use of the Romantic republican movement, but Italian prime minister Camillo di Cavour always intended to establish an enlightened constitutional monarchy that operated with modern pragmatic efficiency. By 1871, Germany also had unified as an empire, instituting the Reichstag, or Imperial Diet, a legislature elected by universal manhood suffrage. Even the autocratic German leader Otto von Bismarck needed to appear receptive to democratic reform. In fact, conservative leaders like Bismarck and British Prime Minister Benjamin Disraeli were remarkable for the extent to which they responded to the needs of the people, establishing some of the first government-sponsored social safety nets.

From the mid-19th century onward, European nation-states in both the east and the west were subject to the influence of the twin movements of Realism and Realpolitik and were increasingly challenged to respond to the desire for enhanced democratic participation and equality. Indeed, the Russian tsar Alexander II understood that an agricultural economy based on serfdom needed to evolve or face extinction. The fight for certain basic rights could be seen in grassroots movements across Great Britain and the Continent in the late 19th and early 20th centuries. Through the trade union movement, despite governmental attempts to constrain it, labour successfully unionized and used its collective strength to push beyond economic concerns for greater political rights. Universal manhood suffrage led to organized demands for women's suffrage, and over time a nascent feminist movement gained followers from all social classes. Urban problems were addressed by religious organizations, like the Salvation Army, that espoused charity and the power of community to resolve deep-rooted issues.

The democratic yearnings of free peoples can appear so universal as to seem inevitable. However, it is important to remember that democracy met with resistance everywhere it grew throughout the modern period. Capitalism and representative democracy threatened governing aristocrats and landed nobles who stood to lose status and advantage. Moreover, democracy was fraught with peril, promising opportunity but offering few safeguards to the masses. As a result, some reformers, including those influenced by the socialist philosopher Karl Marx, sought change in different political and economic forms. Therefore, the history of modern European democracy is also the story of ongoing political and economic challenges. These challenges became increasingly effective, culminating in totalitarian dictatorship in parts of Europe and two world wars in the 20th century. Both World War I and World War II devastated most of Europe for decades, as once-great nations were dwarfed in power, confidence, and influence by the two remaining superpowers: the United States and the Soviet Union.

From 1945 to 1991, Europe was divided by an iron curtain. On either side were nations that defined democracy and the rights of humanity using differing scales and values. After the Cold War subsided and the iron curtain was dismantled, the possibility of an all-encompassing federation of European countries designed to address common problems and goals seemed more attainable. By the end of the 20th century, the foundation of the present-day European Union (EU) had been established, and several European countries had taken preliminary steps in promoting even greater European unity. Despite lingering disparities in their understandings of or approaches to democracy, European countries have been able to reach new compromises with each other and come together on a wide variety of international issues. As the EU expands, the differences that once divided Europe are slowly diminishing, and new understandings are being reached.

Democracy's resulting legacy is impressive when we remember to examine it. Today, across Europe, representative governments, elected by universal suffrage, are judged by their ability to govern for the benefit of all citizens. Free and mandatory public education results in increased opportunities and the expectation of an acceptable standard of living for all citizens. And while societies may haggle over the precise meaning and extent of civil rights, no modern European government would last for long if it denied the legitimacy of these rights for all its citizens. Two hundred years ago, none of these things was true. Modern democracy, "the noble experiment," was a new idea with a limited track record. Today, the world understands and appreciates European democracy's potential to effect positive change and to protect the civil and human rights of all of its citizens.

CHAPTER 1

THE AGE OF REVOLUTION, 1789–1849

Two types of revolution, economic and political, launched the modern era of European history. Beginning in England in the 18th century and continuing throughout Europe in the 19th, the traditional agrarian economy was transformed into one dominated by industry and machine manufacture. The Industrial Revolution, as this process became known, brought to Europe not only profound economic changes but also widespread social upheaval. Meanwhile, a popular social revolution that erupted in France in 1789 had overthrown, albeit temporarily, the French monarchy. The effects of the French Revolution, both political and cultural, reverberated through virtually the entire 19th century.

Some historians prefer to divide 19th-century European history into relatively small chunks. Thus, 1789–1815 is defined by the French Revolution and Napoleon; 1815–48 forms a period of reaction and adjustment; 1848–71 is dominated by a new round of revolution and the unifications of the German and Italian nations; and 1871–1914, an age of imperialism, is shaped by new kinds of political debate and the pressures that culminated in war. Overriding these important markers, however, a simpler division can also be useful. Europe dealt with the forces of political revolution and the first impact of the Industrial Revolution between 1789 and 1849. Then, between 1849 and 1914, a fuller industrial society emerged, including new forms of states and of diplomatic and military alignments.

THE INDUSTRIAL REVOLUTION

Undergirding the development of modern Europe between the 1780s and 1849 was an unprecedented economic transformation that embraced the first stages of the great Industrial Revolution and a still more general expansion of commercial activity. Articulate Europeans were initially more impressed by the screaming political news generated by the French Revolution and ensuing Napoleonic Wars, but in retrospect the economic upheaval, which related in any event to political and diplomatic trends, has proved more fundamental.

Economic Effects

Major economic change was spurred by western Europe's tremendous population growth during the late 18th century, extending well into the 19th century itself. Between 1750 and 1800, the populations of major countries increased between 50 and 100 percent, chiefly as a result of the use of new food crops (such as the potato) and a temporary decline in epidemic disease. Population growth of this magnitude compelled change. Peasant and artisanal children found their paths to inheritance blocked by sheer numbers and thus had to seek new forms of paying labour. Families of businessmen and landlords also had to innovate to take care of unexpectedly large surviving broods. These pressures occurred in a society already attuned to market transactions, possessed of an active merchant class, and blessed with considerable capital and access to overseas markets as a result of existing dominance in world trade.

Heightened commercialization showed in a number of areas. Vigorous peasants increased their landholdings, often at the expense of their less fortunate neighbours, who swelled the growing ranks of the near-propertyless. These peasants, in turn, produced food for sale in growing urban markets. Domestic manufacturing soared, as hundreds of thousands of rural producers worked full- or part-time to make thread and cloth, nails and tools under the sponsorship of urban merchants. Craft work in the cities began to shift toward production for distant markets, which encouraged artisan-owners to treat their journeymen less as fellow workers and more as wage labourers. Europe's social structure changed toward a basic division, both rural and urban, between owners and nonowners. Production expanded, leading by the end of the 18th century to a first wave of consumerism as rural wage earners began to purchase new kinds of commercially produced clothing, while urban middle-class families began to indulge in new tastes, such as uplifting books and educational toys for children.

In this context an outright industrial revolution took shape, led by Britain, which retained leadership in industrialization well past the middle of the 19th century. In 1840, British steam engines were generating 620,000 horsepower out of a European total of 860,000. Nevertheless, though delayed by the chaos of the French Revolution and Napoleonic Wars, many western European nations soon followed suit. Thus, by 1860 British steam-generated horsepower made up less than half the European total, with France, Germany, and Belgium gaining ground rapidly. Governments and private entrepreneurs worked hard to imitate British technologies after 1820, by which time an intense industrial revolution was taking shape in many parts of western Europe, particularly in coal-rich regions such as Belgium, northern France, and the Ruhr area of Germany. German pig iron production, a mere 40,000 tons in 1825, soared to 150,000 tons a decade later and reached 250,000 tons by the early 1850s. French coal and iron output doubled in the same span—huge changes in national capacities and the material bases of life.

Technological change soon spilled over from manufacturing into other areas. Increased production heightened demands on the transportation system to move raw materials and finished products. Massive road and canal building programs were one response, but steam engines also were directly applied as a result of inventions in Britain and the United States. Steam shipping plied major waterways soon after 1800 and by the 1840s spread to oceanic transport. Railroad systems, first developed to haul coal from mines, were developed for intercity transport during the 1820s; the first commercial line opened between Liverpool and Manchester in 1830. During the 1830s local rail networks fanned out in most western European countries, and national systems were planned in the following decade, to be completed by about 1870. In communication, the invention of the telegraph allowed faster exchange of news and commercial information than ever before.

New organization of business and labour was intimately linked to the new technologies. Workers in the industrialized sectors laboured in factories rather than in scattered shops or homes. Steam and water power required a concentration of labour close to the power source. Concentration of labour also allowed new discipline and specialization, which increased productivity.

The new machinery was expensive, and businessmen setting up even modest factories had to accumulate substantial capital through partnerships, loans from banks, or joint-stock ventures. While relatively small firms still predominated, and managerial bureaucracies were limited save in a few heavy industrial giants, a tendency toward expansion of the business unit was already noteworthy. Commerce was affected in similar ways, for new forms

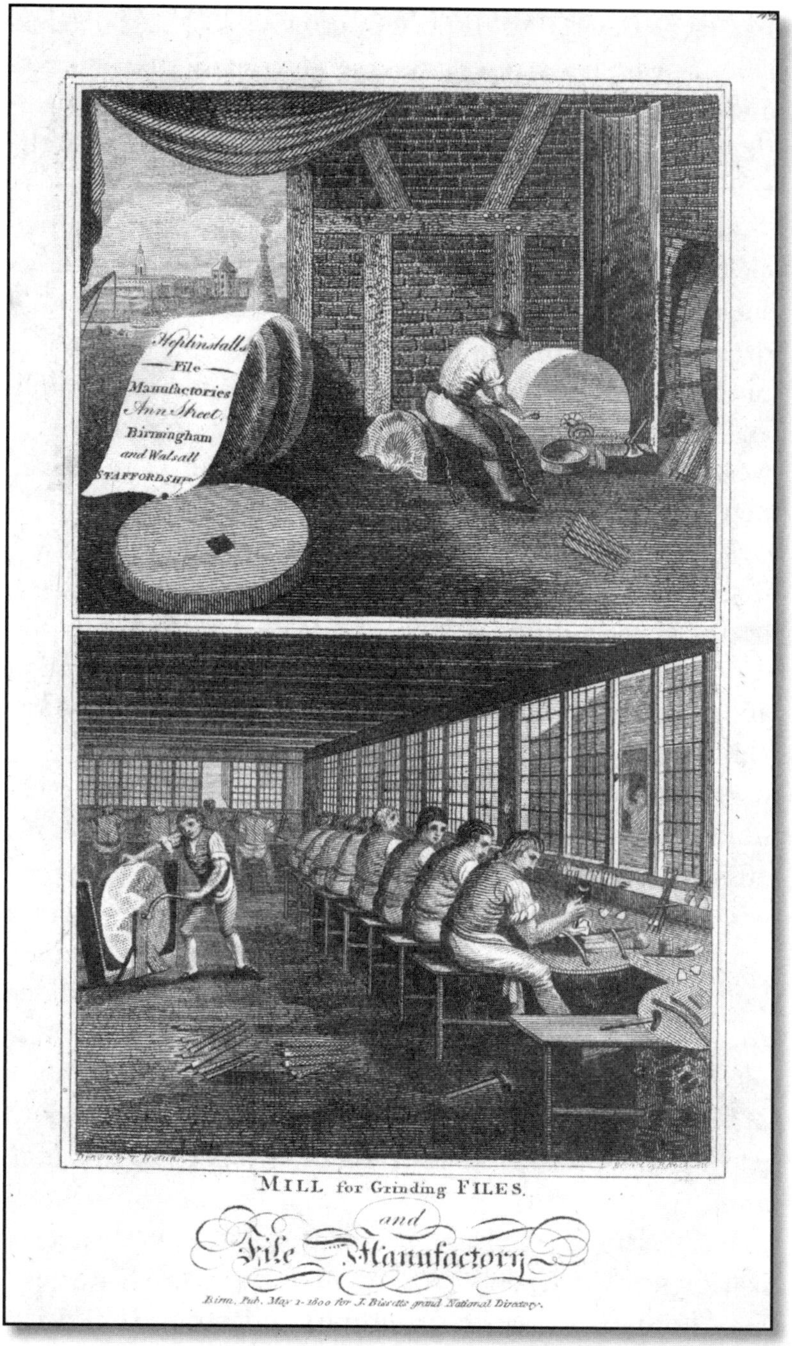

Rendering of workers at a British file factory. SSPL via Getty Images

had to be devised to dispose of growing levels of production. Small shops replaced itinerant peddlers in villages and small towns. In Paris, the department store, introduced in the 1830s, ushered in an age of big business in the trading sector.

Urbanization was a vital result of growing commercialization and new industrial technology. Factory centres such as Manchester grew from villages into cities of hundreds of thousands in a few short decades. The percentage of the total population located in cities expanded steadily, and big cities tended to displace more scattered centres in western Europe's urban map. Rapid city growth produced new hardships, for housing stock and sanitary facilities could not keep pace, though innovation responded, if slowly. Gas lighting improved street conditions in the better neighbourhoods from the 1830s onward, and sanitary reformers pressed for underground sewage systems at about this time. For the better-off, rapid suburban growth allowed some escape from the worst urban miseries.

Rural life changed less dramatically. A full-scale technological revolution in the countryside occurred only after the 1850s. Nevertheless, factory-made tools spread widely even before this time, as scythes replaced sickles for harvesting, allowing a substantial improvement in productivity. Larger estates, particularly in commercially minded Britain, began to introduce newer equipment, such as seed drills for planting. Crop rotation, involving the use of nitrogen-fixing plants, displaced the age-old practice of leaving some land fallow, while better seeds and livestock and, from the 1830s, chemical fertilizers improved yields as well. Rising agricultural production and market specialization were central to the growth of cities and factories.

The speed of western Europe's Industrial Revolution should not be exaggerated. By 1850 in Britain, by and large the leader still, only half the total population lived in cities, and there were as many urban craft producers as there were factory hands. Relatively traditional economic sectors, in other words, did not disappear and even expanded in response to new needs for housing construction or food production. Nevertheless, the new economic sectors grew most rapidly, and even other branches displayed important new features as part of the general process of commercialization.

Geographic disparities complicate the picture as well. Belgium and, from the 1840s, many of the German states were well launched on an industrial revolution that brought them steadily closer to British levels. France, poorer in coal, concentrated somewhat more on increasing production in craft sectors, converting furniture making, for example, from an artistic endeavour to standardized output in advance of outright factory forms. Scandinavia and the Netherlands joined the industrial parade seriously only after 1850.

Southern and eastern Europe, while importing a few model factories and setting up some local rail lines, generally operated in a different economic orbit. City growth and technological change were both modest until much later in the 19th century, save in pockets of northern Italy and northern Spain. In eastern areas, western Europe's industrialization had its greatest impact in encouraging growing conversion to market agriculture, as Russia, Poland, and Hungary responded to grain import needs, particularly in the British Isles. As in eastern Prussia, the temptation was to impose new obligations on peasant serfs labouring on large estates, increasing the work requirements in order to meet export possibilities without fundamental technical change and without challenging the hold of the landlord class.

Social Upheaval

In western Europe, economic change produced massive social consequences during the first half of the 19th century. Basic aspects of daily life changed, and work was increasingly redefined. The intensity of change varied, of course—with factory workers affected most keenly, labourers on the land least—but some of the pressures were widespread.

For wage labourers, the autonomy of work declined; more people worked under the daily direction of others. Early textile and metallurgical factories set shop rules, which urged workers to be on time, to stay at their machines rather than wandering around, and to avoid idle singing or chatter (difficult in any event given the noise of the equipment). These rules were increasingly enforced by foremen, who mediated between owners and ordinary labourers. The pace of work accelerated. Machines set the pace, and workers were supposed to keep up: one French factory owner, who each week decorated the most productive machine (not its operators) with a garland of flowers, suggested where the priorities lay. Work, in other words, was to be fast, coordinated, and intense, without the admixture of distractions common in preindustrial labour. Some of these pressures spilled over to nonfactory settings as well, as craft directors tried to urge a higher productivity on journeymen artisans. Duration of work everywhere remained long, up to 14 hours a day, which was traditional but could be oppressive when work was more intense and walking time had to be added to reach the factories in the first place. Women and children were widely used for the less skilled operations. This was no novelty, but it was newly troubling now that work was located outside the home and was often more dangerous, given the hazards of unprotected machinery.

The nature of work shifted in the propertied classes as well. Middle-class people, not only factory owners but also merchants and professionals, began to trumpet a new work ethic. According to this ethic, work was the basic human good. He who worked was meritorious and should prosper, he who suffered did so because he did not work. Idleness and frivolity were officially frowned upon. Middle-class stories, for children and adults alike, were filled with uplifting tales of poor people who, by dint of assiduous work, managed to better themselves. In Britain, Samuel Smiles authored this kind of mobility literature, which was widely popular between the 1830s and 1860s. Between 1780 and 1840, Prussian school reading shifted increasingly toward praise of hard work as a means of social improvement, with corresponding scorn for laziness.

Shifts in work context had important implications for leisure. Businessmen who internalized the new work ethic felt literally uncomfortable when not on the job. Overall, the European middle class strove to redefine leisure tastes toward personal improvement and family cohesion; recreation that did not conduce to these ends was dubious. Family reading was a common pastime. Daughters were encouraged to learn piano playing, for music could draw the family together and demonstrate the refinement of its women. Through piano teaching, in turn, a new class of professional musicians began to emerge in the large cities. Middle-class people, newly wealthy, were willing to join in sponsorship of certain cultural events outside the home, such as symphony concerts. Book buying and newspaper reading also were supported, with a tendency to favour serious newspapers that focused on political and economic issues and books that had a certain classic status. Middle-class people also attended informative public lectures and night courses that might develop new work skills in such areas as applied science or management.

Middle-class pressures by no means totally reshaped popular urban leisure habits. Workers had limited time and means for play, but many absented themselves from the factories when they could afford to (often preferring free time over higher earnings, to the despair of their managers). The sheer intensity of work constrained leisure nevertheless. Furthermore, city administrations tried to limit other traditional popular amusements, ranging from gambling to animal contests (bear-baiting, cock-fighting) to popular festivals. Leisure of this sort was viewed as unproductive, crude, and—insofar as it massed urban crowds—dangerous to political order. Urban police forces, created during the 1820s in cities like London to provide more professional control over crime and public behaviour, spent much of their time combating popular leisure impulses during the middle decades of the 19th century. Popular habits did not fully accommodate middle-class standards. Drinking, though disapproved of by middle-class critics, was an important recreational outlet, bringing men together in a semblance of community structure. Bars sprouted throughout working-class sections of town. On the whole, however, the early decades of the Industrial Revolution saw a massive decline of popular leisure traditions. Even in the countryside, festivals were diluted by importing paid entertainers from the cities. Leisure did not disappear, but it was increasingly reshaped toward respectable family pastimes or spectatorship at inexpensive concerts or circuses, where large numbers of people paid professional entertainers to take their minds away from the everyday routine.

The growth of cities and industry had a vital impact on family life. The family declined as a production unit as work moved away from home settings. This was true not only for workers but also for middle-class people. Many businessmen setting up a new store or factory in the 1820s initially assumed that their wives would assist them, in the time-honoured fashion in which all family members were expected to pitch in. After the first generation, however, this impulse faded, in part because fashionable homes were located at some distance from commercial sections and needed separate attention. In general, most urban groups tended to respond to the separation of home and work by redefining gender roles, so that married men became the family breadwinners (aided, in the working class, by older children) and women were the domestic specialists.

In the typical working-class family, women were expected to work from their early teens through marriage a decade or so later. The majority of women workers in the cities went into domestic service in middle-class households, but an important minority laboured in factories; another minority became prostitutes. Some women continued working outside the home after marriage, but most pulled back to tasks, such as laundering, that could be done domestically. Their other activities concentrated on shopping for the family (an arduous task on limited budgets), caring for children, and maintaining contacts with other relatives who might support the family socially and provide aid during economic hardships.

Few middle-class women worked in paid employment at any point in their lives. Managing a middle-class household was complex, even with a servant present. Standards of child rearing urged increased maternal attention, and women were also supposed to provide a graceful and comfortable tone for family life. Middle-class ideals held the family to be a sacred place and women its chief agents because of their innate morality and domestic devotion. Men owed the family good manners and the provision of economic security, but their daily interactions became increasingly peripheral. Many middle-class families also began, in the early 19th century, to limit their birth rate, mainly through increasing sexual abstinence. Having too many children could complicate the family's economic well-being and prevent the necessary attention and support for the children who were desired. The middle class thus pioneered a new definition of family size that would ultimately become more widespread in European society.

New family arrangements, both for workers and for middle-class people, suggested new courtship patterns. As wage earners having no access to property, urban workers were increasingly able to form liaisons early in life without waiting for inheritance and without close supervision by a watchful community. Sexual activity began earlier in life than had been standard before the 1780s. Marriage did not necessarily follow, for many workers moved from job to job and some unquestionably exploited female partners who were eager for more durable arrangements. Rates of illegitimate births began to rise rapidly throughout western Europe from about 1780 (from 2 to 4 up to 10 percent of total births) among young rural as well as urban workers. Sexual pleasure, or its quest, became more important for young adults. Similar symptoms developed among some middle-class men, who exploited female servants or the growing numbers of brothels that dotted the large cities (and that often did exceptional business during school holidays). Respectable young middle-class women held back from these trends. They were, however, increasingly drawn to beliefs in a romantic marriage, which became part of the new family ideal. Marriage age for middle-class women also dropped, creating an age disparity between men and women in the families of this class. Economic criteria for family formation remained important in many social sectors, but young people enjoyed more freedom in courtship, and other factors, sexual or emotional or both, gained increasing legitimacy.

Changes in family life, rooted in shifts in modes of livelihood and methods of work, had substantial impact on all family members. Older people gained new roles, particularly in working-class families, where they helped out as baby-sitters for grandchildren. Women's economic power in the family decreased. Many groups of men argued vigorously that women should stick to family concerns. By the 1830s and '40s one result was the inception of laws that regulated women's hours of work (while leaving men free from protection or constraints); this was put forth as a humanitarian move to protect women's family roles, but it also reduced women's economic opportunities on grounds of their perceived frailty. The position of children also began to be redefined. Middle-class ideals held that children were innocents, to be educated and nurtured. Most working-class families urged a more traditional view of children as contributors to the family economy, but they too could see advantages in sending their children to school where possible and restricting their work in dangerous factories. After the first decades of industrialization, reform laws began to respond. Legislation in Britain, France, and Prussia during the 1830s restricted the employment of young children in the factories and encouraged school attendance.

Along with its impact on daily patterns of life and family institutions, economic change began to shift Europe's social structure and create new antagonisms among urban social classes. The key division lay between the members of the middle class, who owned businesses or acquired professional education, and those of the working class, who depended on the sale of labour for a wage. Neither group was homogeneous. Many middle-class people criticized the profit-seeking behaviour of the new factory owners. Artisans often shunned factory workers and drew distinctions based on their traditional prestige and (usually) greater literacy. Some skilled workers, earning good wages, emulated middle-class people, seeking education and acquiring domestic trappings such as pianos.

Nevertheless, the social divide was considerable. It increasingly affected residential patterns, as wealthier classes moved away from the crowded slums of the poor, in contrast to the greater mixture in the quarters of preindustrial cities. Middle-class people deplored the work and sexual habits of many workers, arguing that their bad behaviour was the root cause of poverty. City governments enacted harsh measures against beggars, while new national laws attempted to make charity harder to obtain. The British Poor Law Reform of 1834, in particular, tightened the limits on relief in hopes of forcing able-bodied workers to fend for themselves.

Class divisions manifested themselves in protest movements. Middle-class people joined political protests hoping to win new rights against aristocratic monopoly. Workers increasingly organized on their own despite the fact that new laws banned craft organizations and outlawed unions and strikes. Some workers attacked the reliance on machinery in the name of older, more humane traditions of work. Luddite protests of this sort began in Britain between 1810 and 1820. More numerous were groups of craft workers, and some factory hands, who formed incipient trade unions to demand better conditions as well as to provide mutual aid in cases of sickness or other setbacks. National union movements arose in Britain during the 1820s, though they ultimately failed. Huge strikes in the silk industry around Lyon, France, in 1831 and 1834 sought a living minimum wage for all workers. The most ambitious worker movements tended to emphasize a desire to turn back the clock to older work systems where there was greater equality and a greater commitment to craft skill, but most failed. Smaller, local unions did achieve some success in preserving the conditions of the traditional systems. Social protest was largely intermittent because many workers were too poor or too disoriented to mount a larger effort, but it clearly signaled important tensions in the new economic order.

POLITICAL REVOLUTIONS

During the decades of economic and social transformation, western Europe also experienced massive political change. The central event throughout much of the Continent was the French Revolution (1789–99) and its aftermath. This was followed by a concerted effort at political reaction and a renewed series of revolutions from 1820 through 1848.

Connections between political change and socioeconomic upheaval were real but complex. Economic grievances associated with early industrialization fed into later revolutions, particularly the outbursts in 1848, but the newest social classes were not prime bearers of the revolutionary message. Revolutions also resulted from new political ideas directed against the institutions and social arrangements of the preindustrial order. Their results facilitated further economic change, but this was not necessarily their intent. Political unrest must be seen as a discrete factor shaping a new Europe in conjunction with fundamental economic forces.

The French Revolution

Revolution exploded in France in the summer of 1789, after many decades of ideological ferment, political decline, and social unrest. Ideologically, thinkers of the Enlightenment urged that governments should promote the greatest good of all people, not the narrow interests of a particular elite. They were hostile to the political power of the Roman Catholic Church as well as to the tax exemptions and landed power of the aristocracy. Their remedies were diverse, ranging from outright democracy to a more efficient monarchy, but they joined in insisting on greater religious and cultural freedom, some kind of parliamentary institution, and greater equality under the law. Enlightenment writings were widely disseminated, reaching many urban groups in France and elsewhere. The monarchy was in bad shape even aside from new attacks. Its finances were severely pressed, particularly after the wars of the mid-18th century and French involvement against Britain during the American Revolution. Efforts to reform the tax structure foundered against the opposition of the aristocracy. Finally, various groups in France were pressed by economic and social change: aristocrats wanted new political rights against royal power; middle-class people sought a political voice to match their commercial importance and a government more friendly to their interests; and the peasant majority, pressed by population growth, sought access to the lands of the aristocracy and the church, an end to remaining manorial dues and services, and relief from taxation.

These various discontents came to a head when King Louis XVI called the Estates-General (a representative assembly of the clergy, the nobility, and the remaining majority of the people, known as the Third Estate) in 1789 to consider new taxes. This body had not met since 1614, and its calling released all the pressures building during recent decades, exacerbated by economic hardships resulting from bad harvests in 1787–88. Reform leaders, joined by some aristocrats and clergy, insisted that the Third Estate be granted double the membership of the church and aristocratic estates and that the entire body of Estates-General vote as a unit; they insisted, in other words, on a new kind of parliament. The king yielded, and the new National Assembly began to plan a constitution. Riots in the summer of 1789 included a symbolic attack on the Bastille, a royal prison, and a series of risings in the countryside that forced repeal of the remnants of manorialism and a proclamation of equality under the laws. A Declaration of the Rights of Man and the Citizen trumpeted religious freedom and liberty of press and assembly, while reaffirming property rights. Church lands were seized, however, creating a rift between revolutionary and Roman Catholic sentiment. Guilds were outlawed (in 1791), as the revolution promoted middle-class beliefs in individual initiative and freedom for technological change. A 1791 constitution retained the monarchy but created a strong parliament, elected by about half of France's adult males—those with property.

This liberal phase of the French Revolution was followed, between 1792 and 1794, by a more radical period. Economic conditions deteriorated, prompting new urban riots. Roman Catholic and other groups rose in opposition to the revolution, resulting in forceful suppression and a corresponding growing insistence on loyalty to revolutionary principles. Monarchs in neighbouring countries—notably Britain, Austria, and Prussia—challenged the revolution and threatened invasion, which added foreign war to the unstable mix by 1792. Radical leaders, under the banners of the Jacobin party, took over the government, proclaiming a republic and executing the king and many other leaders of the old regime. The leaders of the republic introduced numerous changes. Governmental centralization increased. The decimal system was introduced. Mass military conscription was organized for the first time in European history, with the argument that, now that the government belonged to the people, the people must serve it loyally. A new constitution proclaimed universal manhood suffrage, and reforms in education and other areas were widely discussed. The radical phase of the revolution brought increasing military success to revolutionary troops in effectively reorganized armies, which conquered parts of the Low Countries (the region now made up of the Netherlands, Belgium, and Luxembourg) and Germany and carried revolutionary laws in their wake. The revolution was beginning to become a European phenomenon.

Jacobin rule was replaced by a more moderate consolidation after 1795, during which, however, military expansion continued in several directions, notably in parts of Italy. The needs of war, along with recurrent domestic unrest, prompted a final revolutionary regime change, in 1799, that brought General Napoleon Bonaparte to power.

The Napoleonic Era

Napoleon ruled for 15 years, closing out the quarter-century so dominated by the French Revolution. His own ambitions were to establish a solid dynasty within France and to create a French-dominated empire in Europe. To this end he moved steadily to consolidate his personal power, proclaiming himself emperor and sketching a new aristocracy. He was almost constantly at war, with Britain his most dogged opponent but Prussia and Austria also joining successive coalitions. Until 1812, his campaigns were usually successful. Although he frequently made errors in strategy—especially in the concentration of troops and the deployment of artillery—he was a master tactician, repeatedly snatching victory from initial defeat in the major battles. Napoleonic France directly annexed territories in the Low Countries and western Germany, applying revolutionary legislation in full. Satellite kingdoms were set up in other parts of Germany and Italy, in

Portrait of Napoleon Bonaparte. Hulton Archive/Getty Images

Spain, and in Poland. Only after 1810 did Napoleon clearly overreach himself. His empire stirred enmity widely, and in conquered Spain an important guerrilla movement harassed his forces. Russia, briefly allied, turned hostile, and an 1812 invasion attempt failed miserably in the cold Russian winter. A new alliance formed among the other great powers in 1813. France fell to the invading forces of this coalition in 1814, and Napoleon was exiled. He returned dramatically, only to be defeated at Waterloo in 1815; his reign had finally ended.

Outside of its many military episodes, Napoleon's regime produced three major accomplishments. First, it confirmed many revolutionary changes within France itself. Napoleon was a dictator, maintaining only a sham parliament and rigorously policing press and assembly. Though some key liberal principles were ignored, equality under the law was for the most part actually enhanced through Napoleon's sweeping new law codes. Hereditary privileges among adult males became a thing of the past. A strongly centralized government recruited bureaucrats according to their abilities. New educational institutions, under state control, provided access to bureaucratic and specialized technical training. Religious freedom survived, despite some conciliations of Roman Catholic opinion. Freedom of internal trade and encouragements to technical innovation allied the state with commercial growth. Sales of church land were confirmed, and rural France emerged as a nation of strongly independent peasant proprietors.

Second, Napoleon's conquests cemented the spread of French revolutionary legislation to much of western Europe. The powers of the Roman Catholic Church, guilds, and manorial aristocracy came under the gun, and the old regime was dead in Belgium, western Germany, and northern Italy.

Third, wider conquests permanently altered the European map. Napoleon's kingdoms consolidated scattered territories in Germany and Italy, and the welter of divided states was never restored. These developments, coupled with resentment at Napoleonic rule, sparked growing nationalism in these regions and also in Spain and Poland. Prussia and Russia, less touched by new ideologies, nevertheless introduced important political reforms as a means of strengthening the state to resist the Napoleonic war machine. Prussia expanded its school system and modified serfdom; it also began to recruit larger armies. Britain was less affected, protected by its powerful navy and an expanding industrial economy that ultimately helped wear Napoleon down, but even in Britain, French revolutionary example spurred a new wave of democratic agitation.

In 1814–15 the victorious powers convened at the Congress of Vienna to try to put Europe back together, though there was no thought of literally restoring the world that had existed before 1789. Regional German and Italian states were confirmed as a buffer to any future French expansion. Prussia gained new territories in western Germany. Russia took over most of Poland (previously divided, in the late 18th century, until Napoleon's brief incursion). Britain acquired some former French, Spanish, and Dutch colonies (including South Africa). The Bourbon dynasty, which had previously ruled France from 1589 to 1792, was restored to the French throne in the person of Louis XVIII, but revolutionary laws were not repealed, and a parliament, though based on very narrow suffrage, proclaimed a constitutional monarchy. The Treaty of Vienna disappointed nationalists, who had hoped for a new Germany and Italy, and it certainly daunted democrats and liberals. However, it was not reactionary, nor

Congress of Vienna

Congress of Vienna, *drawing by Jean-Baptiste Isabey, 1815; in the Louvre, Paris.* Courtesy of the Musée du Louvre; photograph, Archives Photographiques

The Congress of Vienna was the assembly in 1814–15 that reorganized Europe after the Napoleonic Wars. Having begun in September 1814, five months after Napoleon's first abdication, it completed its "Final Act" in June 1815, shortly before the Waterloo campaign and the final defeat of Napoleon. The settlement was the most comprehensive treaty that Europe had ever seen.

Austria, Prussia, Russia, and Great Britain, the four powers chiefly instrumental in the overthrow of Napoleon, had concluded a special alliance among themselves with the Treaty of Chaumont, on March 9, 1814, a month before Napoleon's first abdication. The subsequent treaties of peace with France, signed on May 30 not only by the "four" but also by Sweden and Portugal and on July 20 by Spain, stipulated that all former belligerents should send plenipotentiaries to a congress in Vienna. Nevertheless, the "four" still intended to reserve the real decision making for themselves. Two months after the sessions began, however, Bourbon France was admitted to the "four." The "four" thus became the "five," and it was the committee of the "five" that was the real Congress of Vienna.

Representatives began to arrive in Vienna toward the end of September 1814. Klemens, prince von Metternich, principal minister of Austria, represented his emperor, Francis II. Tsar Alexander I of Russia directed his own diplomacy. King Frederick William III of Prussia had Karl, prince von Hardenberg, as his principal minister. Great Britain was represented by its foreign minister, Robert Stewart, Viscount Castlereagh. When Castlereagh had to return to his parliamentary duties, Arthur Wellesley, 1st duke of Wellington, replaced him, and Lord Clancarty was principal representative after the duke's departure. The restored Louis XVIII of France sent Charles-Maurice de Talleyrand, prince de Bénévent. Spain, Portugal, and Sweden had only men of moderate ability to represent them. Many of the rulers of the minor states of Europe put in an appearance. With them came a host of courtiers, secretaries, and ladies to enjoy the magnificent social life of the Austrian court.

The major points of friction occurred over the disposition of Poland and Saxony, the conflicting claims of Sweden, Denmark, and Russia, and the adjustment of the borders of the German states. In general, Russia and Prussia were opposed by Austria, France, and England, which at one point (Jan. 3, 1815) went so far as to conclude a secret treaty of defensive alliance. The major final agreements were as follows.

For Poland, Alexander gave back Galicia to Austria and gave Thorn and a region around it to Prussia; Kraków was made a free town. The rest of the duchy of Warsaw was incorporated as a separate kingdom under the Russian emperor's sovereignty. Prussia got two-fifths of Saxony and was compensated by extensive additions in Westphalia and on the left bank of the Rhine. It was Castlereagh who insisted on Prussian acceptance of this latter territory, with which it had been suggested the king of Saxony should be compensated; Castlereagh wanted Prussia to guard the Rhine against France and act as a buttress to the new Kingdom of the Netherlands, which comprised both the former United Provinces and Belgium. Austria was compensated by Lombardy and Venice and also got back most of Tirol. Bavaria, Württemberg, and Baden on the whole did well.

Hanover was also enlarged. The outline of a constitution, a loose confederation, was drawn up for Germany—a triumph for Metternich. Denmark lost Norway to Sweden but got Lauenburg, while Swedish Pomerania went to Prussia. Switzerland was given a new constitution.

In Italy, Piedmont absorbed Genoa; Tuscany and Modena went to an Austrian archduke; Parma was given to Marie-Louise, consort of the deposed Napoleon. The Papal States were restored to the pope, Naples to the Sicilian Bourbons.

Valuable articles were agreed to on the free navigation of international rivers and diplomatic precedence. Castlereagh's great efforts for the abolition of the slave trade were rewarded only by a pious declaration.

The Final Act of the Congress of Vienna comprised all these agreements in one great instrument. It was signed on June 9, 1815, by the "eight" (except Spain, who refused as a protest against the Italian settlement). All the other powers subsequently acceded to it.

As a result, the lines laid down by the Congress of Vienna lasted, except for one or two changes, for more than 40 years.

was it punitive as far as France was concerned. Overall, the treaty strove to reestablish a balance of power in Europe and to emphasize a conservative political order tempered by concessions to new realities. The former was remarkably successful, preserving the peace for more than half a century, the latter effort less so.

The Conservative Reaction

Conservatism dominated the European political agenda through the mid-1820s. Major governments, even in Britain, used police agents to ferret out agitators. The prestige of the Roman Catholic Church soared in France and elsewhere. Europe's conservative leader was Klemens, prince von Metternich, chief minister of the Habsburg monarchy.

(The Habsburg dynasty, which had ruled the Holy Roman Empire from the 15th century until the empire's demise in 1806, continued to control a significant collection of lands, including Austria, Hungary, and Bohemia.) Yet Metternich realized the fragility of Habsburg rule, not only wedded to church and monarchy but also, as a polyglot combination of German, Hungarian, and Slavic peoples, vulnerable to any nationalist sentiment. He sedulously avoided significant change in his own lands and encouraged the international status quo as well. He also sponsored congresses at several points through the early 1820s to discuss intervention against political unrest. He was particularly eager to promote conservatism in the German states and in Italy, where Austrian administration of northern provinces gave his regime a new stake.

Nevertheless, in 1820 revolutionary agitation broke out in fringe areas. Risings in several Italian states were put down. A rebellion in Spain was also suppressed, though only after several years, foreshadowing more than a century of recurrent political instability; the revolution also confirmed Spain's loss of most of its American colonies, which had first risen during the Napoleonic occupation. A Greek revolution against Ottoman control fared better, for Greek nationalists appealed to European sympathy for a Christian nation struggling against Muslim dominance. With French, British, and Russian backing, Greece finally won its independence in 1829.

Liberal agitation began to revive in Britain, France, and the Low Countries by the mid-1820s. Liberals wanted stronger parliaments and wider protection of individual rights. They also sought a vote for the propertied classes. They wanted commercial legislation that would favour business growth, which in Britain meant attacking Corn Law tariffs that protected landlord interests and kept food prices (and so wages) artificially high. Belgian liberals also had a nationalist grievance, for the Treaty of Vienna had placed their country under Dutch rule.

Liberal concerns fueled a new round of revolution in 1830, sparked by a new uprising in Paris. The French monarchy had tightened regulation of the press and of university professors, prompting a liberal response. Artisans, eager for more political rights, also rose widely against economic hardship and the principles of the new commercial economy. This combination ended the reign of the Bourbon king, producing a new and slightly more liberal monarchy, an expanded middle-class voting system, and some transient protections for freedom of the press. The new regime also cut back the influence of the church. Revolution spread to some German and Italian states and also to Belgium, where after several years an independent nation with a liberal monarchy was proclaimed. Britain was spared outright revolution, but massive agitation forced a Reform Bill in 1832 that effectively enfranchised all middle-class males and set the framework for additional liberal legislation, including repeal of the Corn Laws and municipal government reform, during the next decade.

Europe was now divided between a liberal west and a conservative centre and east. Russia, indeed, seemed largely exempt from the political currents swirling in the rest of the continent, partly because of the absence of significant social and economic change. A revolt by some liberal-minded army officers in 1825 (the Decembrist revolt) was put down with ease, and a new tsar, Nicholas I, installed a more rigorous system of political police and censorship. Nationalist revolt in Poland, a part of the 1830 movement, was suppressed with great force. Russian diplomatic interests continued to follow largely traditional lines, with recurrent warfare with the Ottoman Empire in an effort to gain territory to the south. Only after 1850 did the Russian regime seriously rethink its adamantly conservative stance.

This pattern could not prevail elsewhere in Europe. Scandinavian governments moved toward increasing liberalism by expanding the power of parliaments, a development that was completed in the late 1840s; the Dutch monarchy did the same. Elsewhere, the next major step resulted once again from a series of revolutions in 1848, which proved to be western Europe's final revolutionary round.

The Revolutions of 1848

After adopting reforms in the 1830s and the early 1840s, King Louis-Philippe of France rejected further change and thereby spurred new liberal agitation. Artisan concerns also had quickened, against their loss of status and shifts in work conditions following from rapid economic change. A major recession in 1846–47 added to popular unrest. Some socialist ideas spread among artisan leaders, who urged a regime in which workers could control their own small firms and labour in harmony and equality. A major propaganda campaign for wider suffrage and political reform brought police action in February 1848, which in turn prompted a classic street rising that chased the monarchy (never to return) and briefly established a republican regime based on universal manhood suffrage.

Revolt quickly spread to Austria, Prussia, Hungary, Bohemia, and various parts of Italy. These risings included most of the ingredients present in France, but also serious peasant grievances against manorial obligations and a strong nationalist current that sought national unification in Italy and Germany and Hungarian independence or Slavic autonomy in the Habsburg lands. New regimes were set up in many areas, while a national assembly convened in Frankfurt to discuss German unity.

The major rebellions were put down in 1849. Austrian revolutionaries were divided over nationalist issues, with German liberals opposed to minority nationalisms; this helped the Habsburg regime maintain control of its army and move against rebels in Bohemia, Italy, and Hungary (in the last case, aided by Russian troops). Parisian revolutionaries were divided between those who sought only political change and artisans who wanted job protection and other gains from the state. In a bloody clash in June 1848, the artisans were put down and the republican regime moved steadily toward the right, ultimately electing a nephew of Napoleon I as president. He, in turn (true to family form), soon established a new empire, claiming the title Napoleon III. The Prussian monarch turned down a chance to head a liberal united Germany and instead used his army to chase the revolutionary governments, aided by divisions between liberals and working-class radicals (including the socialist Karl Marx, who had set up a newspaper in Cologne).

Despite the defeat of the revolutions, however, important changes resulted from the 1848 rising. Manorialism was permanently abolished throughout Germany and the Habsburg lands, giving peasants new rights. Democracy ruled in France, even under the new empire and despite considerable manipulation; universal manhood suffrage had been permanently installed. Prussia, again in conservative hands, nevertheless established a parliament, based on a limited vote, as a gesture to liberal opinion. The Habsburg monarchy installed a rationalized bureaucratic structure to replace localized landlord rule. Metternich had been exiled in 1848, and a new generation of conservatives, eager to compromise with and utilize new political forces rather than oppose them down the line, came to the fore in the Habsburg lands. Finally, some new political currents had been sketched. Socialism, though wounded by the failure of the revolutions, was on Europe's political agenda, and some feminist agitation had surfaced in France and Germany. The stage was set for rapid political evolution after 1850, in a process that made literal revolution increasingly difficult.

The years between 1815 and 1850 had not seen major diplomatic activity on the part of most European powers, Russia excepted. Exhaustion after the Napoleonic Wars combined with a desire to use diplomacy as a weapon of internal politics. Britain continued to expand its colonial hold, most notably introducing more direct control over its empire in India. France and Britain, though still wary of each other, joined in resisting Russian gains in the Middle East. France also began to acquire new colonial holdings, notably by invading Algeria in 1829. Seeds were being planted for more rapid colonial expansion after mid-century, but the period remained, on the surface, rather quiet, in marked contrast to the ferment of revolution and reaction during the same decades.

THE LEGACY OF THE FRENCH REVOLUTION

To make the story of 19th-century culture start in the year of the French Revolution is at once convenient and accurate, even though nothing in history "starts" at a precise moment. For although the revolution itself had its beginnings in ideas and conditions preceding that date, it is clear that the events of 1789 brought together and crystallized a multitude of hopes, fears, and desires into something visible, potent, and irreversible. To say that in 1789 reform becomes revolt is to record a positive change, a genuine starting point. One who lived through the change, the duke de La Rochefoucauld-Liancourt, was even sharper in his vision when (as the story goes) he answered Louis XVI, who had asked whether the tumult outside was a revolt: "No, sire, it is a revolution." In cultural history as in political, significance is properly said to reside in events; that is, in the acts of certain men or the appearance of certain works that not only embody the feelings of the hour but also prevent other acts or works from having importance or effect. To list some examples: the year 1790 saw the appearance of Johann Wolfgang von Goethe's *Faust: A Fragment*, of Edmund Burke's *Reflections on the Revolution in France*, of William Blake's *Marriage of Heaven and Hell*, and of Immanuel Kant's *Critique of Judgment*. In these works are found the Romanticist view of human destiny, of the state, of moral energy, and of aesthetics. The remainder of the decade goes on to show that it belongs to a new age; it gave the world Francisco de Goya's "Caprichos" and the portrait of the Duchess de Alba, Ludwig van Beethoven's *Piano Sonata in C Minor (Pathétique)*, Friedrich Hölderlin's *Hyperion*, the beginning of August Wilhelm von Schlegel and Ludwig Tieck's translation of William Shakespeare into German, Friedrich Schelling's *Nature Philosophy*, Johann Gottfried von Herder's *Letters on the Progress of Mankind*, William Wordsworth and Samuel Taylor Coleridge's *Lyrical Ballads*, Friedrich von Schiller's *Wallenstein*, and Friedrich Schleiermacher's *On Religion: Speeches to Its Cultured Despisers*. These are some of the many evidences of a new direction in thought and culture.

To say, then, that the cultural history of the later modern age—1789 to the present—begins with the French Revolution is to discuss that revolution's ideas rather than the details of its onward march during its first 10 years. These ideas are the recognition of individual rights, the sovereignty of the people, and the universal applicability of this pair of propositions. In politics the powerful combination of all three brings about a permanent state of affairs: "the revolution" as defined here has not yet stopped. The revolution is "dynamic" because it does not simply change rulers or codes of law but also arouses a demand and a hope in every individual and every people. When the daily paper tells of another new nation born by breaking away, violently or not, from some other group, the revolutionary doctrine of the sovereignty of the people may be observed still at work centuries later.

Cultural Nationalism

The counterpart of this political idea in the 19th century is cultural nationalism. The phrase denotes the belief that each nation in Europe had from its earliest formation developed a culture of its own, with features as unique as its language, even though its language and culture might have near relatives. Europe was thus seen as a bouquet of diverse flowers harmoniously bunched, rather than as a uniform upper-class civilization stretching from Paris to St. Petersburg, from London to Rome, and from Berlin to Lisbon—where societies acknowledging the same artistic ideals, speaking French, and taking their lead from the French court and culture could be found. In still other words, the revolutionary idea of the people as the source of power ended the idea of a cosmopolitan Europe.

The "uniform" conception presupposed a class or elite transcending boundaries; the "diverse" implied a number of distinct nations made up of citizens attached to their native soil and having an inborn and exclusive understanding of all that had been produced on it. In each nation it is the people as a whole, not just the educated class, that is deemed the creator and repository of culture. Culture, thus, is not a conscious product fashioned by the court artists of the moment; rather, it is the product of the slow growth of centuries. This view of Europe explains one of the great intellectual forces of the postrevolutionary era—the passion for history. An emotion that may be called cultural populism replaced the devotion to a single horizontal, Europe-wide, and "sophisticated" civilization. These vertical national cultures were "popular" not only in their scope but also in their simplicity.

This new outlook, though propagated by the revolution, began as one of those subdued feelings mentioned earlier, as undercurrents beneath Enlightenment doctrine. In England and Germany especially, a taste developed for folk literature—the border ballads, the legends and love songs of the people, their dialects and superstitions. Educated gentlemen collected and published these materials; poets and storytellers imitated them. Horace Walpole in *The Castle of Otranto*, James Macpherson in *Ossian*, Thomas Chatterton in his forgeries of early verse, and Goethe in his lyrics exploited this new vein of picturesque sentiment. A scholar such as Herder or a poet-dramatist such as Schiller drew lessons of moral, psychological, and philosophical import from the wisdom found in the subculture of *das Volk* (literally, "the people"). The folk or people was not as yet very clearly defined, but the revolution would shortly take care of this omission.

In France, where the revolution occurred, the situation was somewhat different. There were no collectors of border ballads or exploiters of Gothic superstitions. By 1789, France had been the cultural dictator of Europe for more than a century, and it is clear that in England and Germany the search for native sources of art was stimulated by the desire to break the tyranny of the French language and literature. The rediscovery of Shakespeare, for example, was in part a move in the liberation from French classical tragedy and its rigid limitations of subject matter and form.

Simplicity and Truth

Yet cultural nationalism was also the expression of a genuine desire for truth. This in turn implied the release of feelings that the Enlightenment's confidence in the power of reason had tended to suppress. Two 18th-century figures tapped this fount of emotion, Samuel Richardson and Jean-Jacques Rousseau. The novels of Richardson, in which innocent girls are portrayed as withstanding the artful seductions of titled gentlemen, might be said to foreshadow in symbolic form the struggle between high cosmopolitan culture and the new popular simplicity. These novels were best-sellers in France, and Rousseau's *Nouvelle Héloïse* followed in their wake, as did the bourgeois dramas of Denis Diderot, Pierre-Augustin Caron de Beaumarchais's satirical comedies about the plebeian Figaro, and the peasant narratives of Restif de la Bretonne, to mention only the most striking exemplars of the new simplicity.

At the very centre of sophistication the simple life became a fad, with the French court (including Marie-Antoinette) dressing up and playing at the rustic existence of milkmaids and shepherds. However silly the symptoms, the underlying passion was real. It was the periodic urge of complex civilizations to strip off the social mask and recover the happiness imagined as still dwelling among the humble. What was held up to admiration was honesty and sincerity, the strong and pure feelings of people unspoiled by court and city life. Literature therefore came to express an acute sensitivity to scenes of undeserved misfortune, of heroic self-sacrifice, of virtue unexpectedly rewarded—a sensitivity marked by tearfulness, actual or "literary."

This surge of self-consciousness about sophisticated culture has often been confused with an idealization of primitive humans and attributed to Rousseau. But contrary to common opinion, the so-called back-to-nature movement does not at all echo the noble-savage doctrine of the 17th century. Rousseau's attack on "civilization," which evoked such a powerful response in the latent feelings of his contemporaries, goes with a characterization of the savage as stupid, coarse, and amoral. In Rousseau and his abettors, what is preached is the simple life. What nature and the natural really are remains to be found by trial and error—the fit methods and forms of religion, marriage, child rearing, hygiene, and daily work.

Populism

It is easy to see in these beliefs and sentiments (which often passed into sentimentality) additional materials for the populism that the revolution fostered. Revolution, to begin with, is also an urge to simplify. The revolutionary style was necessarily populist—the influential newspaper of the radical journalist Jean-Paul Marat was called *L'Ami du peuple* ("The Friend of the People"). The visible signs that a revolution had occurred included the wearing of natural hair instead of wigs and of common workmen's trousers instead of silk breeches, as well as the use of the title of *citoyen* ("citizen") instead of *monsieur* or any other term of rank. Equality coupled with sincerity and simplicity logically leads to fraternity, just as honest feeling coupled with devotion to the people leads to puritanism: a good and true citizen behaves like a moral person. He is, under the revolutionary principles, a responsible unit in the nation, a conscious particle of the will of the sovereign people, and as such his most compelling obligation is love of country—patriotism.

With this last word the circle of ideas making up the cultural ambient of the French Revolution might seem to be complete. However, in the effort to trace back and interweave the strands of feeling and opinion that make up populism, one must not overlook the first political axiom of revolutionary thought, which is the recognition of individual rights. Their source and extent is a subject for political theory. The recognition of the individual goes with the assertion that his freedom rests on natural law, a potent idea, as those who have witnessed the vast extension of rights far beyond their first, political meaning know. Here the concern is with their cultural role, which can be simply stated: individual rights generate individual*ism* and magnify it. That *-ism* denotes both an attitude and a doctrine, which together amount to a passionate belief: every human being is an object of primary interest to himself and in himself; he is an end in himself, not a means to the welfare of class or state or to other group purposes. Further, the truly valuable part of each individual is his uniqueness, which he is entitled to develop to the utmost, free of oppression from the government or from his neighbours. That is why the state guarantees the citizen rights as against itself and other citizens. Again, this power accrues to him for himself because he is inherently important—not because he is son or father, peasant or overlord, member of a clan or a guild.

These ideas shift the emphasis of several thousand years of social beliefs and let loose innumerable consequences. Individualism lowers the value of tradition and puts a premium on originality; it leads to the now familiar "cult of the new"—in art, manners, technology, and social and political organization. True, the individual soul had long been held unique and precious by Christian theology, but Christian society had not extended the doctrine to every person's mundane comings and goings. Nor were people's practical rights and powers attached to them as human beings but, rather, to their status. Now the human being as such was being officially considered self-contained and self-propelling. It was a new regime, and its name was liberty.

Nature of the Changes

The contents and implications of these powerful words—liberty, equality, and fraternity, individualism and populism, simplicity and naturalness—enable us to delineate the cultural situation of Europe at the dawn of the era under review. Yet these continuing ideas necessarily modified each other and in different times and countries were subject to still other influences.

For example, the active phase of the revolution in France—say, 1789 to 1804—was influenced by the Classical education of most of its public men. They had been brought up on Roman history and the tales of Plutarch's republican heroes, so that when catapulted into a republic of their own making, the symbols and myths of Rome were often their most natural means of expression. The eloquence of the successive national assemblies is full of Roman allusions. Later, when General Bonaparte let it be seen that he meant to rule France, he was denounced in the Chamber as a Caesar; when he succeeded, he took care to make himself consul (a title of the ancient Roman Republic), flanked by two other consuls of lesser rank. The title was meant to show that no Caesar was in prospect.

In the fine arts this Roman symbolism facilitated a thorough change of taste and technique. The former "grand style" of painting had been derived from royal and aristocratic elegance, and its allusions to the ancient Classical past were gentle and distant, architectural and mythological. Now, under the leadership of the painter Jacques-Louis David, the great dramatic scenes of ancient history were portrayed in sharp, uncompromising outlines that struck the beholder as the utmost realism of the day.

In David's *Death of Socrates* and *Oath of the Horatii* civic and military courage are the respective subjects; in his pencil sketches of the victims of the Terror as they were led to execution, reportorial realism dominates; and, in his designs for the setting of huge popular festivals, David, in collaboration with the musicians Étienne-Nicolas Méhul and André-Ernest-Modeste Grétry, provided the first examples of an art in scale with the new populism: the courtly taste for intimate elegance and subtle manners gave way to the more striking, less polished large-scale feelings of a proud nation.

It must be added, however, that except for a few canvases and a few tunes (including the "Marseillaise") the quality of French Revolutionary art was not on a par with its aspirations. Literature in particular showed the limitations under which revolutionary artists must work: political doctrine takes precedence over truth, and the broad effects required to move the masses encourage banality. There is no French poetry in this period except the odes of André de Chénier, whom the revolution promptly guillotined, as it did France's greatest scientist, Antoine-Laurent Lavoisier. The French stage was flourishing but not with plays that can still be read. The revolutionary playwrights only increased the dose of sentiment and melodrama that had characterized plays at the close of the old regime. The aim was to hold up priests and kings to execration and to portray examples of superhuman courage and virtue. Modern operagoers who know the plot of Beethoven's *Fidelio* can judge from that sample what the French theatre of the revolutionary years thrived on. Others can imagine for themselves Molière's *Misanthrope* rewritten so as to make Alceste a pure patriot and hero, undermined by the intrigues of the vile courtier Philinte.

It may seem odd that once the revolution was under way there should be such persistent indignation and protest against courtiers, priests, and kings and such fulsome homage paid to virtue and patriotism. What accounts for it is the difficulty of transforming culture overnight. People have to be persuaded out of old habits—and must keep on persuading themselves. Even politically, the revolution proceeded by phases and experienced regressions. Manners and customs themselves did not change uniformly, as one can see from portraits of Maximilien de Robespierre at the height of his power wearing a short wig and knee breeches, republican and Rousseauist though he was.

Napoleon's Influence

After Bonaparte's coup d'état, tension eased as the high revolutionary ideals dropped to a more workaday level, just as the puritanism was replaced by moral license. The general's expedition to Egypt in 1798 before his self-elevation to power introduced a new style competing with the ancient Roman in costume and furnishings. The Middle East became fashionable and out of the cultural contact came the new science of Egyptology. The Roman idea itself shifted from republic to empire as the successful general and consul Bonaparte made himself into the emperor Napoleon in 1804.

The emperor had an extraordinary capacity for attending to all things, and he was concerned that his regime should be distinguished in the arts. He accordingly gave them a sustained patronage such as a revolutionary party rent by internal struggles could not provide. Napoleon, nonetheless, had tastes of his own, and he had to control public opinion besides. In literature (he had been a poet and writer of novels in his youth), he relished the Celtic legends of *Ossian* and encouraged his official composer Jean-François Lesueur in the composition of the opera *Ossian ou les Bardes*. In painting, he favoured the surviving David and the younger men Antoine-Jean, Baron Gros, and Théodore Géricault, both "realists" concerned with perpetuating the colour and drama of imperial life. But to depict matters of contemporary importance on the stage (except perhaps in the ballet, which was flourishing) did not prove possible, for the stage must present genuine moral conflict if it is to produce great works, and moral issues are not discussable under a political censorship.

The paradox of the Napoleonic period is that its most lasting cultural contributions were side effects and not the result of imperial intentions. Two of these contributions were books. One, François-Auguste-René, viscount de Chateaubriand's *The Genius of Christianity* (1802), was a long tract designed to make the author's peace with the ruler and reinvigorate Roman Catholic faith. The other, Germaine de Staël's *Germany* (1810), was a description of the new and thriving literature, philosophy, and popular culture in Germany. Napoleon prohibited the circulation of the book in France, but its message percolated French public opinion nonetheless. Two other sources of future light were the Idéologues, a group of philosophers who were scientific materialists particularly concerned with abnormal psychology, and Napoleon Bonaparte himself, or rather the figure of Napoleon as seen by his age after Waterloo.

CHAPTER 2

The Early 19th Century: Romanticism and Other Cultural Developments

It has been possible so far to discuss the general shift in the temper of European life without naming fixed points. It sufficed to say "before or after 1789" or "from 1789 to the Napoleonic empire." However, from now on the generations of culture makers and the dates of some of their works must be duly situated, without losing sight of unities and similarities in the onward march of artistic and intellectual movements. If, for example, one considers the poets called Romantic or Romanticist, one finds that Johann Wolfgang von Goethe came to maturity in the 1770s, when the English Romantics were just beginning to be born. Their French, Italian, Russian, Polish, and Spanish counterparts were, in turn, born about the year 1800, when the English were already in mid-career. The same irregularity in the onset of Romanticism is found in the other arts, and it is complicated (at least superficially) by the names given to various movements and persons in the different countries of Europe. Thus, in Germany the term *Romantismus* is applied to only a small group of writers, and Goethe and Friedrich von Schiller are called classic. In Poland and in Russia, classic is likewise the label for the great writers whose characteristics in fact align them with the Romantics elsewhere.

All these accidents of birth and nomenclature can be taken in stride by remembering the patterns found in each country or decade and the reasons for their appearance at that time and place. Within the slightly more than half century between 1789 and 1848, the phenomenon of Romanticism occurred and developed its first phase. Those who made it may have come early or late, belonged to this or that nationality, proved to be originators or synthesizers of existing elements—all such considerations appertain to individual biography or the history of a particular art or nation. What matters in the evolution of European culture considered as a whole is the orchestration of all the voices as they come in to swell the ensemble.

In their studies of society, the Romantics and other thinkers of this period were devoted to the "cause of humanity," but they arrived at politically different conclusions. Sir Walter Scott and Benjamin Disraeli were forerunners of Tory democracy as Edmund Burke was of liberal conservatism. Charles Dickens, a passionate humanitarian, stirred the masses with his examples of the law's stupid cruelty, but he proposed no agency of betterment, content to despise Parliament, the law courts, and the complacency of the wealthy. Honoré de Balzac wrote his huge array of novels as a "social zoology" that was to show what a bloody jungle society becomes without the church and the monarchy to restrain human passions. Stendhal noted the same reality but was more concerned with the free play of individual genius. He resigned himself to the social struggle, provided not too many unintelligent individuals ran the inevitably heavy-handed regimes. Freedom might be found by the happy few through the loopholes of a mixed government such as England's.

Yet despite their differences, early 19th-century thinkers agreed that European society and culture had changed irrevocably and that they would continue to change, either through ongoing revolution or through gradual evolution. The biological theory of evolution, which Charles

Darwin devised during this period, supported that notion, as did other scientific discoveries. Although the social and political upheaval provoked a sense of uncertainty among many Europeans, some found reassurance in philosophy, where the theory of idealism was notable, or in religion, where the revival of traditional religions was accompanied by alternative pursuits of truth, such as positivism and art.

THE ROMANTIC MOVEMENT

The main purport of the Romantic movement is commonly said to be a revolt against 18th-century rationalism and a resulting variety of new attitudes and activities: a turning in upon the self, a love of nature, the rediscovery of the Middle Ages, the cult of art, a taste for the exotic, a return to religion, a fresh sense of history, a yearning for the infinite, a maudlin sentimentality, an overvaluing of emotion as such, a liberal outlook in politics, a conservative outlook, a reactionary outlook, a socialist-utopian outlook, and several other "characteristic features."

It is clear that not all these can be equally true, characteristic, or important, since some contradict the others. At the same time it was inevitable that so sweeping a cultural revolution as Romanticism should contain incompatible elements. For instance, the political opinions enumerated above did in fact win the allegiance of different groups among the Romantic artists and thinkers for a longer or shorter time. But—to take note of other supposed definitions—not all Romanticists returned to religion: Goethe and Hector Berlioz were pantheists; Lord Byron and Heinrich Heine, atheists; and Victor Hugo, a sort of Swedenborgian (a follower of the New Church, founded in the 18th century). As for sentimentality, its occurrence was rather a hangover from the 18th century than a new fashion of feeling, for the Romantic cult of art and of strong emotion goes dead against the weak sentimental mood. Similarly, the taste for history, for the Middle Ages, and for the exotic shows a strong curiosity about the particulars of what is real though ignored by previous conventions. All critics, however, are agreed upon one Romantic trait: individualism. And it is here that the figure of Napoleon plays its cultural role.

Napoleon, or more exactly Bonaparte, the revolutionary general, the overthrower of old monarchies and creator of new national republics, the organizing genius who rescued France from chaos and who held off the reactionary forces leagued against him throughout Europe—that figure is the one that inspired Ludwig van Beethoven's *Eroica* symphony, Balzac's and Stendhal's heroes, and the poems, paintings, and compositions of many others. Here was the model of the new man. He was the self-made man and the man of genius. His career was the manifestation of will and intelligence overcoming the greatest imaginable resistance. He typified the individual challenging the world and subduing it by his genius. A movement that numbered as many artists and geniuses as did Romanticism was bound to find in Napoleon the individual par excellence or, as might be said in modern jargon, a supremely autonomous personality. This perception explains why nearly all the great names of the first half of the 19th century are found on the roster of those who praised Napoleon—from Beethoven and Byron to William Hazlitt and Stendhal and Alessandro Manzoni. Some who were politically his enemies—Sir Walter Scott, for example—nonetheless respected and pondered over the miracle of his achievements. No comparable attention has been paid to the dictators of the 20th century, a fact sufficiently explained by the real difference between them and Napoleon. Stendhal, who as a military *intendant* took part in the Russian campaign of 1812, stated that difference: Napoleon was a man of thought and vision and not merely a successful soldier and politician. In everything he touched, he showed originality of conception, a stupendous grasp of detail in execution, and the utmost speed in acting out his vision. This sequence, translated to other realms, was the very pattern of the artist-creator's imagination. It also seemed the vindication of individualism as a philosophy of life: open the world to the individual and the world will witness marvels unimagined before.

These remarks about Napoleon should convey a sense of the Romantics' attitude toward themselves and their situation. It is true that culturally they stood in opposition to their immediate forebears. All generations do the same, yet it is not always true that out of the conflict comes great art. The Romanticists had an advantage in undergoing or being emotionally close to a quarter century of violent change. Besides being a stimulus, the tumult of battle and political overturns did its share to clear the ground for artistic innovation. When habits and expectations are repeatedly upset and frustrated in the broad public realm, the general mind opens up to novelty offered in other realms. That is one avenue of cultural, stylistic, and emotional change. When Stendhal was expounding Romanticism to the French in 1822, he argued that to go on writing in the Neoclassic vein was "to provide literary pleasure for one's grandfather." His remark was readily understood—at least by his young readers. Mighty events had dug a chasm between past and present, making plain the remoteness of the 18th century.

And yet a paradox remains. When a Romantic artist first published his innovative work—say William Wordsworth with the *Lyrical Ballads* of 1798—he had to wait a good while for a hearing, though he might have expected that readers would share his conviction that the style and forms of 18th-century Neoclassicism were dead.

Already in 1783 William Blake had written of contemporary English verse that "The sound is forced, the notes are few." But these two poets' estimate was, so to speak, the professional's view of the state of the art. The public, no longer the small, concentrated court-and-town coterie, lagged behind this perception. It is a cliché that such artists are ahead of their time. It would be more accurate to say that it is the public which lags behind its own time.

This phenomenon is characteristic of the modern period generally, because through social and educational emancipation the audience for things artistic and intellectual has steadily grown larger. That fact complicates the study of the Romantic movement: When did it conquer public opinion in different countries and why at different times? In England and Germany one can point to the 1790s: Blake, Wordsworth, and Samuel Taylor Coleridge; Goethe (with the first fragment of *Faust*), Schiller, Johann Gottfried von Herder, Jean Paul (Richter), Beethoven, Ludwig Tieck, Wilhelm Heinrich Wackenroder, Friedrich Hölderlin, Friedrich Schelling, Friedrich Schleiermacher, and the rediscovery of William Shakespeare mark the advent of the new age.

In Italy, France, and Russia, the decisive years opened in 1820. They are signalized in Russia by the abundant poetic output of Aleksandr Sergeyevich Pushkin, in Italy by the work of Manzoni and Giacomo Leopardi and by the surrounding discussions of literary theory, and in France by the poems of Alphonse de Lamartine, Alfred-Victor, count de Vigny, Alfred de Musset, Hugo, and Marceline Desbordes-Valmore. The paintings of Eugène Delacroix, the first compositions of Berlioz, and Balzac's *Chouans* show that a new spirit was at work. Finally, in the 1830s, Poland—through its poet and novelist Adam Mickiewicz—and Spain—through the works of Ángel de Saavedra, duke de Rivas, José de Espronceda y Delgado,

Mariano José de Larra, and José Zorrilla y Moral—joined the rest of Europe in its richest artistic flowering since the Renaissance. The leading nations can boast one or more Romantic artists of the first magnitude.

Literature

The fundamental Romantic purpose was to grasp and render the many kinds of experience that Classicism had neglected or had stylized. Romanticism was the first upsurge of realism—exploratory and imaginative as to subject matter and inventive as to forms and techniques. The exploration of reality surveyed both the external world of peoples and places and the internal world of the individual. The Scottish and medieval novels of Sir Walter Scott, beginning with *Waverley* in 1814, illustrate the range of the new curiosity, for Scotland was a "wild" place, outside the centres of civilization, and the Middle Ages were similarly "barbarous" and distant in time. When Lord Byron or François-Auguste-René, viscount de Chateaubriand, went to the Middle East or when Goethe went to Italy, it was not in the tradition of gentlemen's tourism; it was in the spirit of the cultural explorer. Byron, for one, by using "the Isles of Greece" and the Mediterranean as settings for his wildly popular narrative poems, was developing in the Western mind a new interest, a new sense that the "exotic" was as real, as important, as Paris or London. In all these writers, factual detail is essential to the new sort of effect: the scenery is observably true, and so is the history, given through local colour. As Byron said when criticized: "I don't care two lumps of sugar for my poetry, but my costume is correct." Blake, 20 years earlier, had taken a stand against Sir Joshua Reynold's academic doctrine that the highest form of painting depicted the broadest general truth. Said Blake: "To particularize is the only merit."

Particulars, moreover, are all equally proper for the artist, and the use he makes of them is what matters. When Wordsworth and Coleridge sought to revivify English poetry, they hit upon two divergent kinds of subject: Coleridge took superstition and the folk tale and wrote "The Rime of the Ancient Mariner" in the form of an old ballad; Wordsworth took the modern street ballad—a kind of rhymed newspaper—and produced his versified incidents of common life in common speech. In France, where the division of the vocabulary into "noble" and "common" (i.e., unfit for poetry) had been made and recorded in dictionaries, the Romantics led by Hugo used the prohibited words whenever they saw fit. Hugo's verse drama *Hernani* (1830) created a scandal in the audience when the heroine was heard to speak of her handkerchief and when a character did not use a roundabout phrase about "the march of the hours" to say: "It is midnight."

The importance of such details can hardly be exaggerated and can perhaps be best understood by recalling what the rediscovery of Shakespeare meant to the Romantics. His rise from grudging esteem, even in England, to European idolatry by 1830 had a significance beyond the one already mentioned of serving to put down French classical tragedy and, with it, French cultural tyranny. The German scholar, critic, and playwright Gotthold Ephraim Lessing was among the first to use Shakespeare for that purpose, but the arguments in his theatre reviews, called *Hamburgische Dramaturgie*, sprang from critical genius and not mere national resentment. Shakespeare spelled freedom from narrow conventions—the set verse form in couplets, the lofty language and long declamations, the adherence to verse throughout, the exclusion of low characters, comic effects, and violent action—or, in a word, from royal and artistic etiquette.

What the rediscovery and idolization of Shakespeare meant (and not to poets and playwrights alone—witness his enormous influence on Berlioz) was the right of the artist to adapt or invent forms to suit contents, to use words formerly excluded from poetic diction, loosen the joints of grammar and metric (or the canons of any art), follow the promptings of his spirit (tragic or gay, vulgar or mysterious, but in any case venturesome), and see where this emancipation from artificial rules led the muse. There was danger in freedom, as always—the conventions ensure safety. The aim of the Romantic genius, however, was not to play safe or even to succeed; it was to explore and invent, multiply modes of feeling and truth, and thereby breathe new life into a dead or dying culture. The motto was not common sense but courage. This resolve explains why the men who came to worship Shakespeare also rediscovered François Rabelais and François Villon and revalued Benedict de Spinoza, the lone dissenter who had revered a God pervading the cosmos; Benvenuto Cellini, the fearless artist at grips with the principalities and powers; and "Rameau's Nephew," the ambiguous hero of Denis Diderot's posthumous dialogue, a strange figure disturbingly in touch with the dark forces of the creative unconscious.

Drama

With so much feeling astir and so many novel ideas being agitated, it might seem logical to expect a flourishing school of Romantic drama. Yet only a few isolated works, more interesting than irreplaceable, compose the dramatic output of the Romanticists—Percy Bysshe Shelley's *Cenci*, Byron's *Manfred*, and Heinrich von Kleist's brilliant pieces in several genres. Ironically, Shakespeare's new role as emancipator had a curiously paralyzing effect on the theatre down to the middle of the century and beyond. In

England, poet after poet tried his hand at poetic drama, only to fail from too anxious a desire to be Shakespearean. On the Continent, various misconceptions about him and old habits of Classical tragedy prevented a new drama from coming to life. Hugo's plays contained brilliant verse, and their form influenced grand opera (Richard Wagner's no less than Giuseppe Verdi's), but the fact remained: the dramatic quality could be found everywhere in Romanticist art except on the stage.

Reflection on this point suggests that, quite apart from Shakespeare, the very concern of the Romantics with exploring the inner and outer worlds simultaneously hampered playwrights. Perhaps great drama requires that one or the other world be taken as settled so that conflict, which is the essence of drama, develops between a strong new force and a solid resistance. Be that as it may, the Romantics found themselves in an age when both inner and outer worlds were in flux and from that double uncertainty derived their creative impetus.

Painting

This generality holds for the painters as well; their "reality," too, was by no means "given," so that the notation of fresh detail and the study of new means to transmute the visible into art occupied all those who came after Jacques-Louis David. Francisco de Goya led the way in Spain by depicting the vulgarity of court figures and the horrors of the Peninsular War. In England, John Constable painted country scenes with a vividness at first unacceptable to connoisseurs. He had to argue with his patron, Sir George Beaumont, about the actual colour of grass. To prove that it was not of the conventional brownish tint used by academicians, he seized a violin, ran out of the room with it, and laid it on the lawn,

Francisco de Goya's The 3rd of May 1808: The Execution of the Defenders of Madrid *(1814). Goya depicts the brutal suppression by the French of the revolt in Madrid during the Peninsular War, part of the Napoleonic Wars fought on the Iberian Peninsula.* Time & Life Pictures/Getty Images

forcing the unaccustomed eye to perceive the difference between chlorophyll and old varnish. At the same time, Théodore Géricault astonished the Parisians by painting, in harrowing detail, *The Raft of the Medusa*, not an antique and noble subject but a recent event: the survivors of a shipwreck adrift and starving on a raft.

The young Delacroix was emboldened by the example and, inspired also by the work of his English friend Richard Parkes Bonington, began to paint contemporary scenes of vivid realism—e.g., the Turkish massacre of the Greek peasants at Chios. Later, Delacroix was to visit Morocco (exoticism again) and to discover there the secret of coloured shadows and other pre-Impressionist techniques. His English counterpart, J.M.W. Turner, was pursuing the same goal of realistic truth, though along a different path that nonetheless also led to Impressionism—and beyond. When asked one day why he had pasted a scrap of black paper on a portion of his canvas, he replied that ordinary pigment was not black enough. And he added: "If I could find something even blacker, I would use that."

Sculpture and Architecture

No similar transformations of the visual occurred in sculpture or architecture. Antonio Canova and Bertel Thorvaldsen continued to produce figures and busts on Neoclassical lines; and only Antoine-Louis Barye, the great sculptor of animals, and François Rude, the creator of the Marseillaise panel on the Arc de Triomphe, showed any signs of the new passions. As for architecture, it may have been the love of history that prevented distinctive work. A.W. N. Pugin and Eugène-Emmanuel Viollet-le-Duc did grasp the principles of what a new style should be, the former's love of Gothic reinstating the merit of framework construction and the latter's breadth of vision as a restorer leading him to predict that iron construction would one day pass from mere utility to high art.

It was actually in railway construction that the seeds of a new architecture were sown. Tunnels and bridges and terminals were needed as early as the mid-1830s, and unassuming engineers—such as Sir Marc Isambard Brunel and his son, Isambard Kingdom Brunel, as well as Robert Stephenson—set to work to design them. All they had for solving the new and awkward problems of topography, speed, and cost were the ideas they drew from machinery and the vulgar materials, chiefly wood and iron, that they had learned how to handle in industry. The results were often remarkable, and they remained to inspire the makers of 20th-century steel and concrete architecture.

Music

It may seem as if the art of music by its nature would not lend itself to the exploration and expression of reality characteristic of Romanticism, but that is not so. True, music does not tell stories or paint pictures, but it stirs feelings and evokes moods, through which various kinds of reality can be suggested or expressed. It was in the rationalist 18th century that musicians rather mechanically attempted to reproduce stories and subjects in sound. These literal renderings naturally failed, and the Romanticists profited from the error. Their discovery of new realms of experience proved communicable in the first place because they were in touch with the spirit of renovation, particularly through poetry. What Goethe meant to Beethoven and Berlioz and what German folk tales and contemporary lyricists meant to Carl Maria von Weber, Robert Schumann, and Franz Schubert are familiar to all who are acquainted with the music of these men.

There is, of course, no way to demonstrate that Beethoven's *Egmont* music—or, indeed, its overture alone—corresponds to Goethe's drama and thereby enlarges the hearer's consciousness of it, but it cannot be an accident or an aberration that the greatest composers of the period employed the resources of their art for the creation of works expressly related to such lyrical and dramatic subjects. Similarly, the love of nature stirred Beethoven, Weber, and Berlioz, and here too the correspondence is felt and persuades the listener that his own experience is being expanded. The words of the creators themselves record this new comprehensiveness. Beethoven referred to his activity of mingled contemplation and composition as *dichten*, making a poem; and Berlioz tells in his *Mémoires* of the impetus given to his genius by the music of Beethoven and Weber, by the poetry of Goethe and Shakespeare, and not least by the spectacle of nature. Nor did the public that ultimately understood their works gainsay their claims.

It must be added that the Romantic musicians—including Frédéric Chopin, Felix Mendelssohn, Mikhail Glinka, and Franz Liszt—had at their disposal greatly improved instruments. The beginning of the 19th century produced the modern piano, of greater range and dynamics than theretofore, and made all wind instruments more exact and powerful by the use of keys and valves. The modern full orchestra was the result. Berlioz, whose classic treatise on instrumentation and orchestration helped to give it definitive form, was also the first to exploit its resources to the full, in the *Symphonie fantastique* of 1830. This work, besides its technical significance just mentioned, can also be regarded as uniting the characteristics of Romanticism in music: it is both lyrical and dramatic, and, although it makes use of a "story," that use is not to describe the scenes but to connect them; its slow movement is a "nature poem" in the Beethovenian manner; the second, fourth, and fifth movements include "realistic" detail of the most vivid kind; and the opening one is an introspective reverie.

Portrait of Romantic composer Frédéric Chopin, painted in 1838 by his contemporary in painting, Eugène Delacroix. Bridgeman Art Library/Redferns/Getty Images

Self-Analysis

In this Romantic investigation of the self, some critics have seen little more than excessive ego or, in modern terms, a tiresome narcissism. No doubt certain Romantic works arouse boredom or disgust with hairsplitting analysis. The boredom, however, is often due to the fact that after a hundred years the discoveries have staled. When fresh, they came as a revelation. In the works of the great poets and novelists, in Hazlitt's essays and Jean Paul's fictions, and the irony of Byron's letters or Heine's journalism, the truth has not grown dim or platitudinous.

It was in any case desirable that this extensive analysis of the self should be attempted then, for only an age in which individualism was both theoretical and passionate could see the logic of the undertaking and act upon it. The logic was this: given the autonomous and unique individual, a search by himself into his moods, motives, fears, and loves must bring forth data otherwise unobtainable. Add these results together, and one has a repertoire of clues to the inner life of humankind as a whole. For the uniqueness of each individual is bounded by traits he shares with his fellows, and this common element enables the psychologist to connect and organize the reports of the self-searchers. It is on this hypothesis, incidentally, that the demand for originality in art has continued unabated since the Romanticists. Forget the "model," for there is no such thing; avoid conformity; discover your true self, the buried child; be authentic and sincere—these precepts, which still govern art and criticism, are the legacy of Romantic individualism.

Introspection naturally implies an inner life worth looking into, and most Romantic artists brought forth extraordinary findings. They form the groundwork of modern thought. One cannot easily imagine Sigmund

Freud or James Joyce, much less the degree of self-consciousness shared by Westerners today, without the deliverances of Blake, Wordsworth, John Keats, Leopardi, Stendhal, Benjamin Constant, Charles-Augustin Sainte-Beuve, Heine, and innumerable other writers of the early 19th century. And towering above them as the creator of the prototype of Romantic introspection is Goethe with his Faust.

Faust was the figure in which a whole age recognized its mind and soul, and the adjective Faustian, as the 20th-century German philosopher Oswald Spengler's use of it made clear, still describes tendencies at work in culture today. The principal one, already mentioned, self-consciousness—the identity crisis—remains. The belief, moreover, that movement or activity is better than repose and that striving is better than achieving is clearly the great postulate of contemporary civilization. Faust himself ends by giving his life to practical works in behalf of his fellow man; however, he sets himself on that path only after a slow and deep analysis of his divided soul, which has been ruled in turn by despair, lust, superstition and the forces of the unconscious, the love of innocence, the conviction of sin and crime, the horrors of hypocrisy and conventional life, the temptations of wealth and power, the disgust with pedantry and established religion, and the yearning for infinite knowledge, in the hopes of attaining by it wisdom and peace. Faust, in short, traverses the whole cosmos, made up of the inner and outer worlds, to find in the act of self-dedication to humanity the justification of his existence.

SOCIAL AND POLITICAL THOUGHT

Behind all 19th-century writings on politics and society lay the shadow of the French Revolution. In the 1790s the

Faust

Faustus, illustration by Edwin Austin Abbey. Photos.com/Jupiterimages

Faust, also called Doctor Faustus, is the hero of one of the most durable legends in Western folklore and literature. It is the story of a German necromancer or astrologer who sells his soul to the devil in exchange for knowledge and power. There was a historical Faust, indeed perhaps two, one of whom more than once alluded to the devil as his *Schwager*, or crony. One or both died about 1540, leaving a tangled legend of sorcery and alchemy, astrology and soothsaying, studies theological and diabolical, necromancy and, indeed, sodomy. Contemporary references indicate that he was widely traveled and fairly well known, but all observers testify to his evil reputation. Contemporary humanist scholars scoffed at his magical feats as petty and fraudulent, but he was taken seriously by the Lutheran clergy, among them Martin Luther and Philippe Melanchthon. Ironically, the relatively obscure Faust came to be preserved in legend as the representative magician of the age that produced such occultists and seers as Paracelsus, Nostradamus, and Agrippa von Nettesheim. The publication of magic manuals bearing Faust's name became a lucrative trade. The books included careful instructions on how to avoid a bilateral pact with the devil or, if need be, how to break it. The classic of these, *Magia Naturalis et Innaturalis*, was in the grand-ducal library in Weimar, Ger., and was known to Johann Wolfgang von Goethe.

The German writer Gotthold Lessing undertook the salvation of Faust in an unfinished play (1780). Lessing, an enlightened rationalist, saw Faust's pursuit of knowledge as noble and arranged for the hero's reconciliation with God. This was the approach also adopted by Goethe, who was the outstanding chronicler of the Faust legend.

Goethe's verse drama *Faust* (Part I, 1808; Part II, 1832) makes of the Faust myth a profoundly serious but highly ironic commentary on the contradictory possibilities of Western cultural heritage. The play, which contains an array of epic, lyric, dramatic, operatic, and balletic elements, ranges through various poetic metres and styles to present an immensely varied cultural commentary that draws upon theology, mythology, philosophy, political economy, science, aesthetics, music, and literature. In the end Goethe saves Faust by bringing about his purification and redemption.

Hector Berlioz was moved to create a dramatic cantata, *The Damnation of Faust*, based upon the French version of Goethe's dramatic poem by Gerard de Nerval. This work, first performed in 1846, is also staged as an opera. Charles Gounod based his opera *Faust* on Part I of the Goethe work, with a libretto by Jules Barbier and Michel Carré. It was first performed in Paris in 1859.

Faust was the figure in which the Romantic age recognized its mind and soul. The character, in his self-consciousness and crisis of identity, has continued to appeal to writers through the centuries.

revolution had aroused Burke to write his famous *Reflections* and Joseph de Maistre his *Considérations sur la France*. They differed on many points, but what both saw, like their successors, was that revolution was self-perpetuating. There is no way to stop it because liberty and equality can be endlessly claimed by group after group that feels deprived or degraded. And the idea that these principles are universally applicable removes any braking power that national tradition or circumstance might afford.

Postrevolutionary Thinking

Proof that the revolution marched on, slow or fast, could be read (as it still can be) in every issue of the daily paper since 1789. In the early 19th century the greatest pressure came from the liberals, whether students, bankers, manufacturers, or workmen enlisted in their cause. They wanted written constitutions, an extension of the suffrage, civil rights, a free-market economy, and from time to time wars of national liberation or aggrandizement in the name of cultural and linguistic unity. For example, all the intellect of western Europe sided with Greece in the 1820s when it began its war of emancipation from Turkey. Byron himself died at Missolonghi while helping the Greeks. Poets wrote odes that musicians set to music, and painters painted scenes of war. Between this liberalism and the nationalism that sought freedom from foreign rule the line could not be clearly drawn. In Italy, Germany, Poland, Russia, Spain, Portugal, and South America, revolt in the name of liberty was endemic until the middle of the century. Only England escaped by a timely reform of Parliament in 1832, but it averted revolution only by a hair's breadth, after protracted threats of civil war and many violent incidents expressing the same animus as elsewhere.

Meanwhile, the first disturbances resulting from machine industry—sabotage, strikes, and conspiracies (for trade unions were generally held illegal)—reinforced the revolutionary momentum, not only in fact but also in theory. As early as 1810 the business cycle, the doctrine of the exploitation of the worker, and the degradation of life in industrial societies had been noted and discussed. By 1825 the writings of Henri de Saint-Simon, which proposed a reorganization of society to cure these evils, had won adherents; by 1830 the Saint-Simonians were an acknowledged party with sympathizers abroad, and by 1832 the words "socialism" and "socialist" were in use.

The Saint-Simonians proposed a benevolent dictatorship of industrialists and scientists to remove the inequities of the free-for-all liberal system. Other reformers, such as the practical Robert Owen, who organized successful communities in Scotland and the United States, depended on a strong leader using ad hoc methods. Still others, such as Pierre Leroux and Étienne Cabet, were communists of divergent kinds seeking to carry out elaborate blueprints of the perfect state. Pierre-Joseph Proudhon denounced the state, as such, and all private property. As a philosophical anarchist, he wished to substitute free association and contract for all legal compulsions. In England, the school of Jeremy Bentham and John Stuart Mill—utilitarians or philosophical radicals—attacked existing institutions in the name of the greatest good for the greatest number, and by their arguments they succeeded in reforming the top-heavy legal system. Without doctrine but moved by a similar sense of wrong, Thomas Carlyle fought the utilitarians for their materialistic expediency and himself sought light on the common problem by pondering the lessons of the French Revolution and publishing in 1837 what is still the greatest account of its catastrophic course. Later, Carlyle gave in *Past and Present* a suggestive picture of what he deemed a true community: quasi-medieval, based on the Faustian joy of work, and relying for its cohesion on its leader's genius and strength of soul.

In the Germanies, repeated outbreaks did little to change the system imposed from Vienna by Klemens, prince von Metternich—censorship, spying on students and intellectuals, and repression of group activities at the first sign of political or social advocacy. This drove original thought underground or abroad in the persons of refugees such as the poet Heine, and later, Karl Marx. At home, the prevailing mood was despair. Max Stirner in his book *The Ego and His Own* (1845) recommended, instead of social reform, a ruthless individualism that should seek satisfaction by any means and at whatever risk. A small group of other individualists, Die Freien ("The Free"), found satisfaction of the ego through total disillusion and radical repudiation: nothing is true or good—the state is a monster, society sheer hypocrisy, religion a fraud, for God is dead (1840).

Elsewhere the struggle went on, taking shape as reform or revolt as occasion arose. In Italy and France, secret societies carried out propaganda for programs that might be liberal, nationalist, or socialist, but all revolutionary. One irony about the socialists is that the tag that has clung to them is utopian. It suggests purely theoretical notions, whereas the historical fact is that a great many were tried out in practice, and some lasted for a considerable time. As in Carlyle's book, the force of character of one man (Owen was a striking example) usually proved to be the efficient cause of success. Throughout this social theorizing, whatever the means or ends proposed, two assumptions hold: one is that individuals have a duty to change European society, to purge it of its evils; the other is that individuals can change society—they need only come together and decide what form the change shall take. These axioms by themselves, without the memory of 1789, were enough to keep alive in European culture the hope and the threat of continuing revolution.

The Principle of Evolution

Yet it should not be imagined that revolution by force or radical remodeling inspired every thinking European. Even if liberals and reactionaries were still ready to take to the barricades to achieve their ends, the conservatives were not, except in self-defense. The conservative philosophy, stemming from Burke and reinforced by modern historical studies, maintained the contrary principle of evolution. Evolution indeed swayed as many 19th-century minds as its rival, and it was sometimes the same minds.

Evolution was the belief that lasting and beneficial change comes about by slow and small degrees. It is often imperceptible and therefore congenial to human habits. It breaks no heads and spills no blood; it is natural and organic. The idea of evolution is patterned on biology—the slow growth and decay of living things. More than that, evolution in the zoological sense of "descent with modification" had been a recognized speculation among men of science since 1750, when Georges-Louis Leclerc, count de Buffon, included it in his *Histoire naturelle*. Jean-Baptiste Lamarck had elaborated the idea at the turn of the 18th century, while Erasmus Darwin, the grandfather of Charles, had by 1796 worked out for himself a compendious theory of similar import. In 1830–33 the geologist Charles Lyell, setting forth the corresponding notion that changes in the Earth take place through the operation of constant and not cataclysmic causes, devoted a chapter to Lamarckian biology—to the evolution of species by imperceptible steps.

As if these teachings were not enough to implant a form of thought, the revival of interest in history made easy and obvious the transition from the world of nature to that of society. It seemed logical to think of both as evolutions and even to liken the state to an organism. Certainly the student of institutions finds them steadily and profoundly altered by minute incidents and variations. Compared to these causes, the violent breaks made by war and revolution seem more superficial and less permanent.

The evolutionary scheme encouraged several other beliefs while also furnishing fresh arguments and convenient principles. Anyone who had inherited from the previous era a faith in progress could now attach it to this new motive power, evolution. Anyone who wished to classify nations or institutions by rank could place them as he thought proper on an evolutionary scale. Anyone who resisted change or wished to speed it up could be admonished with the aid of some evolutionary yardstick. Finally, anyone who intended to write a work of history or propaganda found the organizing principle ready-made. In the first half of the 19th century, every subject of interest, from costume to the criminal law, was presented in innumerable studies as proceeding majestically at an evolutionary pace.

Another way of stating the influence of this great idea is to say that the mind of Europe had experienced the "biological revolution." Whereas in the 17th century Newtonian physics and its description of the cosmos had imposed the model of mechanics and mathematics, what impressed itself on the 19th century as the universal pattern was the living organism—change and variety as against fixity and regularity. The logic of preferring "biology" to "mechanics" in an age of individualism, of realism about concrete particulars, and of passionate imagination and introspection need only be stated to be evident.

SCIENCE

This is not to say that the science of physics stood still during the Romanticist period. It was the time when the conservation of energy was established and the mechanical equivalent of heat demonstrated. There also prevailed the "physical" pseudo-science of phrenology, which professed to relate individual attributes to bumps and hollows in the skull and which led to the physical anthropology that defined 3, 10, 20, and 100 different races of humans by the end of the century. Still, the 19th was more emphatically the century that furnished the theory of the cell (Mathias Jacob Schleiden and Theodor Schwann, 1838–39), which led ultimately to the notion of microscopic creatures responsible for putrefaction and disease and, later still, to cytology and genetics.

It is noteworthy, too, that the 19th century saw the establishment of chemistry on John Dalton's hypothesis of the atom, but it was coloured by the "biological" notion of elective affinities to explain compounds. Goethe, who was an early evolutionist and the scientific expositor of the metamorphosis of plants, called his last novel of human love *Elective Affinities*.

On the surface the poetic mind of the age seemed hostile to both science and technology. Wordsworth looks like an enemy of science when he says: "We murder to dissect" and deprecates the man who is willing to "peep and botanize upon his mother's grave." Yet reflection shows that the animus here is not so much against science in general as for the science of life and the reality of human thought and feeling. To understand this temper of the times one must remember how uncertain the intellectual status of physical science still was. Eighteenth-century philosophy had ended in materialism and skepticism. Some writers, such as Paul-Henri Dietrich, baron d'Holbach, had reduced all phenomena to the interaction of hard and unfeeling particles; others, such as David Hume, had "proved" that humans can know nothing beyond their impressions and therefore can have no certainty about the truth of cause and effect, on which scientific statements depend. The Romanticist generations could neither agree that life was a concourse of unfeeling atoms nor trust the physicists' assertions based on a law of causation that the most acute thinkers had discredited.

Such were the iron constraints within which the famous "crises of the soul" and conversions to religions new or old took place in the 1820s and '30s. Carlyle, Mill, Félicité Lamennais, and many others described these crises in famous autobiographical works. The choice seemed to be between a blind and meaningless universe and human life conceived as a brief, pointless exception to the mechanical play of forces. Even if the latter scheme "explained," it was vulnerable to Hume's irrefutable doubts.

PHILOSOPHY

What enabled 19th-century culture to pursue the scientific quest and regain confidence in spiritual truth was the work of the German idealist philosophers, beginning with Immanuel Kant. Kant took up Hume's challenge that it is impossible to know anything about the world beyond one's own impressions. He showed that, although we may never know "things as they are," we can know truthfully and reliably the data of experience. The reason for this certitude is that the mind imposes its categories of time and space and causation on the flowing stream and gives it shape. Science, therefore, is not a guess, nor is human knowledge a dream. Both are solid and verifiable. Indeed, certainty, according to Kant, extends as far as morals and aesthetics. The essence of morals is the commandment not to perform any act that one would not want to become a precedent for all human action and always to consider an individual as an end in himself, not as the instrument of another's purpose. The fusion in Kant of ideas stemming from Jean-Jacques Rousseau and the Enlightenment with ideas fitting the needs of the coming century (Kant died in 1804) made him the fountainhead of European philosophy for 50 years.

Idealism

In metaphysics, or the philosophical study of reality, the theory of idealism stresses the central role of the ideal or the spiritual in the constitution of the world and in humankind's interpretation of experience. Idealism may hold that the world or reality exists essentially as spirit or consciousness, that abstractions and laws are more fundamental in reality than sensory things, or, at least, that whatever exists is known to humankind in dimensions that are chiefly mental—that is, through and as ideas. Metaphysical idealism asserts the ideality of reality; epistemological idealism holds that in the knowledge process the mind can grasp only its own contents. Metaphysical idealism is thus directly opposed to materialism (the doctrine that physical matter is the only, or fundamental, reality), and epistemological idealism is opposed to realism (the viewpoint that the objects of human knowledge have an existence that is independent of whether they are being perceived or thought about). Absolute idealism, as conceived by Georg Wilhelm Friedrich Hegel, includes the following principles: (1) the everyday world of things and persons is not the world as it really is but merely as it appears in terms of uncriticized categories; (2) the best reflection of the world is in terms of a self-conscious mind; (3) thought is the relation of each particular experience with the infinite whole of which it is an expression; and (4) truth consists in relationships of coherence between thoughts, rather than in a correspondence between thoughts and external realities.

His disciples—Johann Gottlieb Fichte, Georg Wilhelm Friedrich Hegel, Arthur Schopenhauer—twisted or amplified his teachings. Coleridge in England and Victor Cousin in France adapted to home use what seemed fitting. The school as a whole was known as German idealism because it relied on the distinction between the thinking subject and the perceived object; "idea" and "thing" were unlike, but idea (or the mind) played a role in shaping the reality of things, from which derived all stability and regularity in the universe.

Stability was desirable as a guarantor of natural science, but in the social world it was obviously contradicted by events, especially by those since the French Revolution. By 1840 many historians had told the story of the past 50 years, and the lesson they drew from it was almost uniformly that of pessimism. Deprived of Providence and the explanation it used to supply by its "mysterious workings," history seemed neither morally rational nor humanly tolerable.

The German philosopher Hegel, however, drew a different conclusion. Coming after Kant and having witnessed Napoleon's victory at Jena in 1806, he conceived the world as ruled by a new logic, no longer a logic of things static but of things in movement. He saw the forces of history in perpetual battle. Neither side wins, but the upshot of their struggle is an amalgam of their rival intentions. Hegel called the pros and the cons and their survivors thesis, antithesis, and synthesis. Human affairs are ever in dialectic (dialoguing) progression. At times a "world-historical figure" (Martin Luther, Napoleon) embodies the aspirations of the masses and gives them effect through war, revolution, or religious reformation. Yet throughout the succession of events, what is taking place is the unfolding of Spirit or Idea taking on itself the concrete forms of the real. Hegel's was another version of evolution and progress, for he foretold the extension of liberty to all men as the fulfillment of history. It is interesting to note that until 1848 or 1850 Hegel was generally considered a dangerous revolutionary, a believer in an irresistible progress that humankind must earn by blood and battle. Karl Marx, as a younger Hegelian, was to carry out Hegel's unspoken promise on a different base.

Other branches of the all-powerful German philosophy deserve attention but can be spoken of only as they relate to high Romantic themes. Fichte's modification of Kant made the ego the "creator" of the world, an extreme extension or generalization of individualism. At the other extreme, but more in tune with contemporary science and art, Schelling made nature the source of all energy, from which individual consciousness takes off to become the observer of the universe. Nature is a work of art and the individual is, so to say, its critic, and because human consciousness results from an act of self-limitation, it perceives moral duty and feels the need to worship.

RELIGION AND ITS ALTERNATIVES

That need made itself felt ecumenically throughout Europe from the beginning of the 19th century. It had indeed been prepared by the writings of Rousseau as early as 1762 and in England by the even earlier preaching of John and Charles Wesley, the founders of Methodism. The surviving atheism and materialism of the 18th-century philosophes was in truth a greater stimulus to the religious revival of the early 19th century than anything the French Revolution had done, briefly, to replace the established religions. When in the 1800s the Roman Catholic writings of Chateaubriand and Lamennais in France, the neo-Catholic Tractarian movement in England, and the writings of Schleiermacher and his followers in Germany began to take effect, their success was due to the same conditions that made Romanticist art, German idealism, and all the "biological" analogies succeed: the great thirst caused by dry abstractions in the Age of Reason needed quenching. Religious fervour, artistic passion, and "gothic" systems of philosophy filled a void created by the previous simple and mechanical formulas.

The religious revivals, Catholic or Protestant, also aimed at political ends. Their participants feared the continuation in the 19th century of secularism and wholly material plans. In every country the liberals proposed to set up in the name of tolerance ("indifference," said the Christian believers) governments that would serve exclusively practical (indeed commercial) interests. Church and state were to be separated, education was to be secular, which would really mean antireligious. National traditions would be broken, forgotten, and youth would grow into "economic man," Benthamite utilitarian man, with no intuition of unseen realities, no sensitivity to art or nature, no humility, and no inbred morals or sanction for their dictates.

Scientific Positivism

This desire for renewed faith and passion, however, found alternative goals. One was scientific positivism; the other was the cult of art. The name "positivism" is the creation of Auguste Comte, a French thinker of a mathematical cast of mind who in 1824 began to supply a philosophy of the natural sciences opposed to all metaphysics. Science, according to Comte, delivers unshakable truth by limiting itself to the statement of relations among phenomena. It does not explain but describes—and that is all humankind needs to know. From the physical sciences rise the social and mental sciences in regular gradation (Comte coined the word "sociology"), and from these humans will learn, in time, how to live in society.

Having elaborated this austere system, Comte discovered the softer emotions through a woman's love, and he amended his scheme to provide a "religion of humanity" with the worship of secular saints, under a political arrangement that the sympathetic Mill nonetheless described as "the government of a beleaguered town." Comte did not attract many orthodox disciples, but the influence of his

The father of sociology and originator of positivism, Auguste Comte. Hulton Archive/Getty Images

positivism was very great down to recent times. Not alone in Europe but also in South America it formed a certain type of mind that survives to this day among some scientists and many engineers.

The Cult of Art

The second "religious" alternative, the cult of art, has had even greater potency, being at the present time the main outlet for spirituality among Western intellectuals. In the Romantic period this fervour was allied with the love of nature and the idolatrous admiration of the man of genius, beginning with Napoleon. A writer as sober as Scott, a thinker as cogent as Hegel, and an artist as skeptical as Berlioz could all say that to them art and its masters were a religion, and they were not alone. At the death of Goethe in 1832, Heine inveighed against the great man's followers who made art the only reality. In the second and third Romantic generations, born about 1820, the religion of art grew still more pronounced and took on an antisocial tone that became more and more emphatic as time passed. "Art for art's sake" ended by signifying, among other things, "art the judge of society and the state." This doctrine was expounded in full detail by the Romantic poet Théophile Gautier as early as 1835 in the preface to his entertaining and sexually daring novel *Mademoiselle de Maupin*. In those pages the familiar argument against bourgeois philistinism, practical utility, the prevailing dullness, ugliness, and wrongness of daily life was set forth with much wit and a spirit of defiance that one usually thinks of as belonging to the 1890s or the present day. Its occurrence then is but another proof that Romanticism was the comprehensive culture from which later styles, thoughts, and isms have sprung.

CHAPTER 3

The Mid-19th Century: Realism and Realpolitik

The middle decades of the 19th century loom as a particularly important period of transition. During the half century when Romanticism was deploying its talents and ideas, the political minds inside or outside Romanticist culture were engaged in the effort to settle—each party or group or theory in its own way—the legacy of 1789. There were at least half a dozen great issues claiming attention and arousing passion. One was the fulfillment of the revolutionary promise to give all Europe political liberty—the vote for all men, a free press, a parliament, and a written constitution. Between 1815 and 1848 many outbreaks occurred for this cause. Steadily successful in France and England, they were put down in central and eastern Europe under the repressive system of Metternich.

A second issue was the maintenance of the territorial arrangements of the treaties that closed the Napoleonic Wars at the Congress of Vienna in 1815. The spies and generals under Klemens, prince von Metternich, also worked to keep this part of the post-Napoleonic world intact; that is, the boundaries that often linked (or separated) national groups in order to buttress dynastic interests. Except in Belgium, the surge of national, as distinct from liberal, aspirations throughout Europe was unsuccessful in the 1830s. Defeats only strengthened resolve, particularly in Germany and Italy, where the repeated invasions by the French during the revolutionary period had led to reforms and stimulated alike royal and popular ambitions. In these two regions, liberalism and nationalism merged into one unceasing agitation that involved not merely the politically militant but the intellectual elite. Poets and musicians, students and lawyers joined with journalists, artisans, and good bourgeois in open or secret societies working for independence: they were all patriots and all more or less imbued with a Romanticist regard for the people as the originator of the living culture, which the nation was to enshrine and protect.

To be sure, this patriotic union of hearts did not mean agreement on the details of future political states, and the same disunion existed to the west, in England and France, where liberals, only half satisfied by the compromises of 1830 and 1832, felt the push of new radical demands from the socialists, communists, and anarchists. Reinforcing these pressures was the unrest caused by industrialization—the workingman's claims on society, expressed in strikes, trade unions, or (in England) the Chartists' demanding "the Charter" of a fully democratic Parliament. This cluster of parties agitated for a change that went well beyond what the advanced liberals themselves had not yet won. Add to these movements those that purposed to stand still or to restore former systems of monarchy, religion, or aristocracy, and it is not hard to understand why the great revolutionary furnace of 1848–52 was a catastrophe for European culture. The four years of war, exile, deportation, betrayals, coups d'état, and summary executions shattered not only lives and regimes but also the heart and will of the survivors. The hoped-for evolution of each nation and would-be nation, as well as the desire for a Europe at peace, was broken and, with all other hopes and imaginings, rendered ridiculous. The search began for new ways to achieve, on the one side, stability and, on the opposite, the final desperate revolution that would usher in the good society.

For although they seemed decisive, the battles of 1848 and after did not, in fact, test the worth of any one idea. Nationalism won and lost in different parts of Europe. Liberalism gained in Italy and Switzerland, but was set back in Germany and France. English Chartism seemed to collapse, yet its demands began to be carried out. The socialist experiment in France (Louis Blanc's national workshops) also seemed discredited; yet the ensuing regime of Napoleon III made attempts, however clumsy, to deal with poverty by welfare methods. There was peace, but war was imminent, and subversive groups continued to plot and frighten the bourgeois, to try to kill royal heads of state, while machine industry and the resulting urbanization contributed their gains at the cost of the now familiar miseries and sordor.

In these circumstances the mind of Europe suffered an eclipse, followed by a protracted mood of despondency. Many established or emerging artists and thinkers had been killed or torn from their homes or deprived of their livelihood: Richard Wagner fleeing Dresden, where he conducted the opera; Frédéric Chopin and Berlioz at loose ends in London, because in Paris music other than opera was moribund; Giuseppe Verdi going back to Milan with high patriotic hopes and returning to Paris in a few months, utterly disillusioned; and Hugo in exile in Belgium and later in Guernsey—all typify the vicissitudes in which men of reputation found themselves in mid-career. For the young and unknown, such as the poet Charles Baudelaire or the English painters who formed the Pre-Raphaelite Brotherhood, it was no time to invite the public to admire boldness and accept innovation. Critics and public alike were all nerves and hostility to subversion. To read Gustave Flaubert's masterpiece, *Sentimental Education* (1869), is to understand the atmosphere in which the first phase

Realpolitik

Politics based on practical objectives rather than on ideals—in other words, a reaction to things as they are, rather than how they should be—are known as Realpolitik. Realpolitik suggests a pragmatic, no-nonsense view and a disregard for ethical considerations. In diplomacy it is often associated with relentless, though realistic, pursuit of the national interest.

of Romanticism ended and its ramified sequels came into being.

The dominant feeling was that high hopes had perished in gunfire, and this realization bred the thought that hope itself was an error. Any new effort must therefore stay close to the possible, the "real." Realism with a capital "R" (referring to the 19th-century artistic and philosophical movement) and Realpolitik together sink their roots in a distrust of human imagination. This grim caution born of harsh experience coincided with a sense of fatigue that made Romanticist work seem like the foolishness of youth.

The appropriate cultural note must no longer be the infinite or heroic or colourful but rather their opposites. If the commonly accepted term "Realism" for this reaction of the 1850s is used, it must be with these presuppositions in mind. For the Romantic passion for the particular and exact was a type of realism, too. It was what Samuel Johnson much earlier had called "vehement real life." The Realism of the disillusioned 1850s dropped the vehement and the passionate and, in order to run no risk of further disillusion, limited what it called real to what could be readily seen and felt: the commonplace, the normal, the workaday, and often the sordid.

In the same spirit Realpolitik rejected principles. The word did not mean "real" in the English sense; in German it connotes "things"—hence a politics of adaptation to existing facts, pursuing plain objects, admitting no obligation to ideals. In this light we can understand the unexpected epithet "scientific" that Karl Marx and his followers bestowed on their brand of socialism. It was a science not merely because it was presumably based on the laws of history but even more because in its view the advent of the socialist state was to result from the interaction of things (classes, means of production, and economic necessity) and not, as in earlier socialism, from the will (that is, the imaginative efforts of thinking men). The "objective" appearance given to the new politics of things, socialist or other, generated that tough, no-nonsense atmosphere, which people then wanted as a source of reassurance in all their dealings.

SCIENTIFIC MATERIALISM

This search for certainty went with a swinging back of the pendulum in science itself from the vitalism of the previous period to the materialism of the mid-century. German philosophers derided idealism and taught the equivalence of consciousness and chemistry: "without phosphorus, no thinking." The machine once more became the great model of thought and analogy—and nowhere more vividly and persuasively than in biology, where Charles Darwin's advocacy of natural selection won the day because it provided a mechanical means for the march of evolution. The struggle for life (Herbert Spencer's phrase of 1850, adopted by Darwin in the subtitle of his book) obviously had the requisite "toughness" to convince and, like Realpolitik, it followed no principle—whoever survived survived. That Darwin to the very last included other factors in his theory of evolution—Jean-Baptiste Lamarck's "use and disuse" as well as direct environmental forces—carried no weight with a generation bent upon machine certainty. These secondary explanations were ignored, in the usual way of cultural single-mindedness, and for 30 years after the publication of Darwin's *Origin of Species* in 1859, an orthodoxy of universal mechanism reigned over all departments of thought.

It prevented the recognition of Gregor Mendel's work on genetics; it put religious, philosophical, and ethical thought on the defensive—only what was "positive" (i.e., material) held a presumption of being real and true. The same reasoning produced a school of social Darwinists who saw war between nations and economic struggle among individuals as beneficent competition leading to the survival of "favoured races"—another phrase from Darwin's subtitle. And by a final twist of logic, the creed of materialism reinforced the moral gloom of the period by casting doubt on both the permanence and the validity of all that was being redefined as "really real." For on the one side, the second law of thermodynamics guaranteed the cooling of the Sun and the pulverization of the cosmos into cold and motionless bits of matter; and, on the other, orthodox "machine-ism" brought its leading prophets, T.H. Huxley and John Tyndall, to consider people and animals as automatons moved as helplessly as atoms and planets. Consciousness is an epiphenomenon—in plain words, an illusion—precisely as in Karl Marx's writings, which claim that consciousness and culture are illusions floating above the reality of economic relations.

VICTORIAN MORALITY

To be sure, not everybody in Europe believed or worried about these affirmations. And although ideas long debated do in the end filter down to the least intellectual layers of the population, the time and place of triumph for a philosophy are limited by this cultural lag—a fortunate delay, without which whole societies might collapse soon after the publication of a single book. What kept mid-19th-century civilization whole was a subdued faith in the reality of all the things Realism and materialistic science denied: religious belief, civic and social habits, the dogma of moral responsibility, and the hope that consciousness and will did exist.

The sum of these invisible forces is conveniently known as the Victorian ethos or Victorian morality, a formula applicable to the Continent as well as Britain and one whose meaning antedates not only the mid-century revolutions but also the accession of Queen Victoria in 1837. Like Romanticism, this powerful moralism had its roots in the late 18th century—in Wesleyan Methodism and the Evangelical movement, in Rousseau, Schiller, and Kant. Its earnestness was of popular origin; it was anti-aristocratic in manners, and it sought the good and the true in a simple, direct, unhesitating way. Perceiving with warm feeling that all men are brothers under God, the moral person saw that slavery was wrong and, having so concluded, proceeded to have it abolished by act of Parliament (Britain, 1833).

Such fervent convictions when widely shared exert tremendous power, and this concentration of belief and emotion made Victorian morality long impregnable. As the early 20th-century critic G.K. Chesterton said of the Victorian painter George Frederick Watts:

> *He has the one great certainty which marks off all the great Victorians from those who have come after them: he may not be certain that he is successful, or certain that he is great, or certain that he is good, or certain that he is capable: but he is certain that he is right.*

The sense of rightness generated a sense of power, which the Victorians applied to the monumental task of keeping order in a postrevolutionary society.

Partly by taking thought and partly by instinct, they perceived that the drive to revolution and the sexual urge were somehow linked. Therefore they repressed sexuality; that is, repressed it in themselves and their literature, while containing it within specified limits in society. Further, they knew that the successful working of the vast industrial machine required a strict, inhuman discipline. The idolatry of respectability was the answer to natural waywardness. To pay one's bills, wear dark clothes, stifle individual fancy, go to church regularly, and turn aggression upon oneself in the form of worry about salvation became the approved common modes of pursuing the pilgrimage of life.

It could not be expected that everybody would or could conform. From its beginning to the end, the Victorian age numbered a galaxy of dissenters and critics who scorned the conformity, called the religion a sham, and viewed respectability as mere hypocrisy. Yet the front held, and the massed forces behind it were at their strongest after the multiplied assaults of 1848.

Nothing gives a better idea of the astonishing moral structure called Victorianism than the development of the London Metropolitan Police, begun under Sir Robert Peel in 1829. A lawyer and a former captain who had fought in the Peninsular War were the first joint commissioners and creators of the force. At first they had to weed out the drunks and the bullies who had been the main types of recruit in earlier attempts at policing cities. At first, too, the people both ridiculed and fought with the new police. Gradually, the "peelers" came to be trusted; they remained unarmed regardless of circumstances; they learned to handle rioters without shedding blood; and in the putting down of crime they finally enlisted the public on their side. For something less than a century this unique relationship lasted, in which "law-abiding" and "police" were terms of respect—correlative terms, since the peelers (later "bobbies") could not have become what they were without the self-discipline and moral cohesion of the "respectable."

"Peelers," as the members of Robert Peel's London Metropolitan Police force came to be called, were often mocked and disparaged as this editorial cartoon suggests. They were eventually able to earn the public's respect by upholding a moral Victorian sensibility throughout the city. Hulton Archive/Getty Images

The upheavals of the mid-century, cultural as well as political, put Victorianism to a severe test, for after wars and civil disorders laxity is natural, and ensuing despair induces a reckless fatalism. There was cause indeed for apprehension. When the Great Exhibition of 1851 was planned on a scale theretofore unattempted, many expressed the fear that to allow tens of thousands from all over Europe to come together under the Crystal Palace was to invite massive riots. Ministers and heads of state would be assassinated. In the event, no protracted assembly of common people and their leaders was ever so quiet and orderly. The moral machinery worked as efficiently as that which was on display under the glass dome.

THE ADVANCE OF DEMOCRACY

Yet, while a stringent moralism held in check endemic subversion and anarchy, Darwinism and the machine analogy stimulated endless forms of self-consciousness. If people could fashion and continually improve these engines, perhaps they could also engineer an improved society. Because evolution was at last "proved," thanks to Darwin, perhaps it also gave warrant for social and political progress by gradual steps. Spencer's all-inclusive philosophy, likened then to Aristotle's, foresaw an inevitable movement from the simple and undifferentiated to the complex and specialized—as in modern life. Clearly, thought and purpose were common to all people, and among evolutionists and scientific socialists alike, thought and purpose included the hastening by voluntary action of what was sure to come by force of natural laws. These and other desires acting in the light of Realism and taking shape in the increasing organization of the toiling masses brought Europe to accept democracy as inevitable.

The word "democracy" is used here in a cultural sense. It does not imply a set of political institutions so much as the signs and the agencies that herald the coming populist state of our day: for example, the extension of the franchise, in parliamentary or plebiscite form; the secret ballot; the legalization of trade unions; the rise of a Roman Catholic social movement; the passage of education acts providing free, public, and compulsory schooling; the formulation of the paternalistic Tory democracy as a cure for the evils of free-for-all economic liberalism; the beginnings of welfare legislation (in France under Napoleon III, in Germany under Otto von Bismarck); the secularization of life by state action, by the prestige of science, and also by the liberal movements within the churches themselves; and finally, after a decade or so of public education, the great extension and popularization of the press. At the passage of the Reform Act of 1867 in Britain, which gave the vote to urban workingmen, Robert Lowe had said, "Now we must educate our masters." In a parliamentary system the means to that education cannot be the schools alone. The adult "common man" must continually be informed and appealed to for his own satisfaction as well as for coherent policy in government. The instrument for this purpose was the new journalism. The quarterlies of the early 19th century gave way to the monthlies in the 1860s and they in turn to the weeklies, while the daily papers, costing now but a penny and simplifying all they touched, began to reach the millions.

REALISM IN THE ARTS

In the period of so-called Realism, the arts and philosophy as usual supplied—at least for the educated elite—form

Realism

In the arts, realism is the accurate, detailed, unembellished depiction of nature or of contemporary life. Realism rejects imaginative idealization in favour of a close observation of outward appearances. As such, realism in its broad sense has comprised many artistic currents in different civilizations. In the visual arts, for example, realism can be found in ancient Hellenistic Greek sculptures accurately portraying boxers and decrepit old women. The works of such 17th-century painters as Caravaggio, the Dutch genre painters, the Spanish painters José de Ribera, Diego Velázquez, and Francisco de Zurbarán, and the Le Nain brothers in France are realist in approach. The works of the 18th-century English novelists Daniel Defoe, Henry Fielding, and Tobias Smollett may also be called realistic.

Realism was not consciously adopted as an aesthetic program until the mid-19th century in France, however. One of the first appearances of the term "realism" was in the publication *Mercure français du XIXe siècle* in 1826, in which the word is used to describe a doctrine based not upon imitating past artistic achievements but upon the truthful and accurate depiction of the models that nature and contemporary life offer the artist. Between 1850 and 1880, Realism—capitalized when referring to the 19th-century movement—was a major trend in French novels and paintings. The French proponents of Realism were agreed in their rejection of the artificiality of both the Classicism and Romanticism of the academies and on the necessity for contemporaneity in an effective work of art. They attempted to portray the lives, appearances, problems, customs, and mores of the middle and lower classes, of the unexceptional, the ordinary, the humble, and the unadorned. Indeed, they conscientiously set themselves to reproducing all the hitherto-ignored aspects of contemporary life and society—its mental attitudes, physical settings, and material conditions.

Realism was stimulated by several intellectual developments in the first half of the 19th century. Among these were the anti-Romantic movement in Germany, with its emphasis on the common people as an artistic subject; Auguste Comte's positivist philosophy, in which sociology's importance as the scientific study of society was emphasized; the rise of professional journalism, with its accurate and dispassionate recording of current events; and the development of photography, with its capability of mechanically reproducing visual appearances with extreme accuracy. All these developments stimulated interest in accurately recording contemporary life and society.

and substance to the prevailing fears and desires. The mood of soberness and objectivity was alone acceptable, and what art presented to the public confirmed the reasonableness of the mood.

Literature

This interaction accounts for such things as the marked change of tone in Dickens's novels that occurs between *David Copperfield* (1850) and *Bleak House* (1853). The temper expressed in most concentrated form the very next year in *Hard Times* now dominates Dickens's mind and works to the end: life is a dreary sort of underworld; happy endings are artificially contrived and not to be believed.

The same mood explains why Flaubert's *Madame Bovary* (1857), which ranks today as the Realistic novel par excellence and is on all counts grim enough in its rendering of boredom and vulgar misery, was judged "too artistic" by some contemporary critics, not close enough to the most common of realities, that of common speech. At the same time, the sought-for effect could be achieved in poetry by juxtaposing the ideal, or simply the decent, with the

Gustave Flaubert, French Realist novelist. AFP/Getty Images

dreary and disgusting, especially the occurrence of these in the now hateful urban life. This is what Baudelaire did in a volume of poems called *The Flowers of Evil* (1857). The attack this time came not from critics who found the work insufficiently real, but from the "respectable" readers who found it indecent and immoral.

Yet the evolution of Flaubert's mind remains instructive for an understanding of Realism as a literary creed. Flaubert had begun by writing a highly coloured, imaginative story, *The Temptation of Saint Anthony* (1848), which the author's friends advised him to burn, tone down, or rewrite. Flaubert put it aside and began the novel that became *Madame Bovary*. Its setting was the provincial world around him, not the Egyptian desert; the characters were of the most ordinary type, not an improbable

Christian ascetic haunted by visions. Yet, even in the working out of his plain tale, Flaubert had to subdue his lyrical Romantic genius to the discipline he had adopted. The description of a rainstorm, for instance, had to be done over and over again so that it would not stand out and be "interesting" by virtue of the observer's mind. It had to be made ordinary and the observer kept outside, just as in science. *Madame Bovary*, begun as a magazine serial, was soon censored by the editor and then prosecuted as immoral by the state. For Flaubert's Realism had gone so far as to portray in no flattering colours the dreary lives and motives of average provincials of both sexes, and the picture violated the rules of the indispensable moralism. What is more, the fate of Flaubert's unhappy heroine symbolized what had happened to the more daring, poetic, and glorious time before 1848: as Flaubert said, Emma Bovary was himself.

His novel is thus simultaneously a model and a critique of the new genre—a critique, too, of the state of Europe that produced it. Many other writers between 1850 and 1890 pursued matter-of-factness without this ulterior effect and rendered the details of middling life with such impassiveness and fidelity that to this day many use "realistic" as a synonym for dreary or sordid and regard "the novel" as a reliable historical source. On the precise definition of Realism, George Gissing gave, through a character in one of his own novels, a brilliant commentary: the character is at work on a novel which shall be so true to the dullness of daily life that no one will be able to read it.

Painting and Sculpture

The term Realism applies no less to the plastic arts than to literature, but in painting and sculpture it proved difficult to give form overnight to the change of attitude just noticed in literature and political life. The transition between the passionate poetry and drama of Théodore Géricault and Eugène Delacroix and the Realism of Gustave Courbet and Édouard Manet was gradual. It came by way of the "open-air" school of Barbizon, whose landscapes seemed arid (at least to the classically trained academic painters of the day) and pointless in the sense

Édouard Manet's Portrait of M. and Mme. Auguste Manet, *1860. Manet's portrait of his parents reflects the starkness exhibited in many Realist paintings.* Peter Willi/SuperStock/Getty Images

that they depicted the commonplace. Still, when the full shock of Realism inflicted by the works of Courbet and Manet occurred, it was severe: here were coarseness and violence in manner and subject. Courbet's backgrounds are thick and his people drab; Manet's nude *Olympia* is no goddess nor even a beautiful woman; she is a prostitute, and her name seems ironic. The portrait of his parents is

Detail of Gustave Courbet's The Artist's Studio, a Real Allegory of a Seven-Year Long Phase of My Artistic Life, *1855, showing Courbet himself seated at the easel.* Time & Life Pictures/Getty Images

a painful representation of simple poverty unrelieved by any glow of spirit or intelligence—yet the work itself is beautiful: such was, throughout, the aim and achievement of Realism.

In England, by an historical accident, pictorial realism was embodied in subjects that seem far removed from the commonplace. The school that took up the challenge against academic painting and modified the vision of John Constable and J.M.W. Turner called itself Pre-Raphaelite. Its members were Holman Hunt, John Millais, and Dante Gabriel Rossetti, and the name they took for their "brotherhood" expressed their resolve to paint like the masters who came before the imitators of Raphael. It is necessary to put it in this clumsy way in order to make clear that Raphael himself was not being condemned, only his academic followers who introduced "unreality."

To be a Pre-Raphaelite was to see the world with a sharp eye and an undistorting mind and to render it with intense application to solidity of form, bright colour, and natural pose and grouping. All this was to be understood from the motto "Death to Slosh!" In order to make the new virtues vividly clear and also because the Pre-Raphaelites were reared on great literature, their subjects tended to draw upon legend, or Dante Alighieri, or the New Testament. It was the conception and treatment that constituted the innovation. Everybody could see it, because it went against the habit of "pretty-pretty" illustration. In fact the nominal subject dropped out of sight in the startled response to form and colour. Paradoxically, then, the commonplace subjects of the French Realists and the legendary ones of the English Pre-Raphaelites were alike insignificant when compared with the effort to re-create by art the texture and "feel" of actuality—and nothing more. Such was precisely the goal Flaubert pursued and reached in *Madame Bovary*. His final version of the St. Anthony story (1874) employed a legendary subject, as did the Pre-Raphaelites, to make the same point.

Popular Art

It hardly needs to be added that this conscious purpose of high art could interest but a relatively small portion of the public and that, for the growing mass of readers of fiction and viewers of art, other kinds of satisfaction were necessary. The ordinary three-volume novel from the lending library and the continued serial in the magazine or newspaper supplied the demand by aping, adapting, and diluting not one but half a dozen literary tendencies, old and new. The number of novels produced in all languages in the 19th century has never been estimated, but it surely must be on the order of astronomical magnitudes. And the whole output was realistic in the sense that it professed to impart the real truth about life. It was contemporary in setting and speech, took the form of a history, and taught its readers how other people lived. The pictorial counterpart was the "chromo," the cheap colour lithograph that illustrated either fiction or news stories in forms which, however false they must seem to a critical eye, again gave the illusion of commonplace reality.

Music

At first sight, it would seem as if music were a medium in its nature resistant to Realism, but that is to overlook the obvious use that music has always made of sounds directly associated with life—church bells, hunting horns, military bands, and the like. In an age when Realism was

German composer and theorist Richard Wagner. Hulton Archive/Getty Images

at a premium, the opera would be the form where these and other associations easily found their place. So it was in mid-century Europe, where Giacomo Meyerbeer and others provided the effects to suit the fussily "real" staging of all plays, musical or not. Clocks, tables, animals, waterfalls, and especially costumes could be relied on to be genuine up to the limits of the possible: live bullets for real deaths were shied away from, and real lightning was out of reach.

A genius who is often mistakenly grouped with the Romantics, Wagner, supplied this ultimate deficiency—and by musical means. As critics have pointed out, Wagner's system of leitmotivs, or musical tags that denoted an object, a person, or an idea, was consciously or unconsciously an accommodation of Realist intent to operatic understanding. This is true not simply because the musical notes "wave" up and down as Isolde waves her scarf at Tristan—a trivial enough device of a sort found in many composers; it is also true in the deeper sense, which constitutes Wagner's unique genius, namely that he was able to compose great music that was steadily and precisely denotative of items in the story by repeating and interweaving their assigned musical tags.

Summary

Viewed through the filter of the Modernism that would succeed it in the 20th century, Romanticism did not stop in the middle of the 19th. Rather, it evolved and branched out into the phases known as Realism, Neoclassicism, Naturalism, and Symbolism. All the tendencies and techniques that gave passing unity to these actions and reactions are found in germ in the original flowering of art and thought that dates from about 1790.

By concentrating on one purpose, by specializing as it were in one affirmation, the succeeding movements after 1848 made their emphatic mark, until the original inspiration was exhausted. It is thus that cultural movements end—in sterile imitation and pointlessness—and thereby earn the scorn of the next generation. This in turn explains why in the decade before World War I one finds, besides a fresh surge of energy and shocking creations, the driving force of anti-Romanticism, anti-Victorianism, anti-everything that was not some form of the new and "Modern."

CHAPTER 4

A Maturing Industrial Society, 1849–1914

As during the previous half century, much of the framework for Europe's history from about 1850 was set by rapidly changing social and economic patterns, which extended to virtually the entire continent. In western Europe, shifts were less dramatic than they had been at the onset of the Industrial Revolution, but they posed important challenges to older traditions and to early industrial behaviours alike. In Russia, initial industrialization contributed to revolutionary tensions soon after 1900.

THE "SECOND INDUSTRIAL REVOLUTION"

The geographic spread of the Industrial Revolution was important in its own right. Germany's industrial output began to surpass that of Britain by the 1870s, especially in heavy industry. The United States became a major industrial power, competing actively with Europe. American agriculture also began to compete as steamships, canning, and refrigeration altered the terms of international trade in foodstuffs. Russia and Japan, though less vibrant competitors by 1900, entered the field, while significant industrialization began in parts of Italy, Austria, and Scandinavia. These developments were compatible with increased economic growth in older industrial centres, but they did produce an atmosphere of rivalry and uncertainty even in prosperous years.

Throughout the most advanced industrial zone (from Britain through Germany) the second half of the 19th century was also marked by a new round of technological change. New processes of iron smelting, such as that involving the use of the Bessemer converter (invented in 1856), expanded steel production by allowing more automatic introduction of alloys and in general increased the scale of heavy industrial operations. The development of electrical and internal combustion engines allowed transmission of power even outside factory centres. The result was a rise of sweatshop industries that used sewing machines for clothing manufacturing; the spread of powered equipment to artisanal production, construction sites, bakeries and other food-processing centres (some of which saw the advent of factories); and the use of powered equipment on the larger agricultural estates

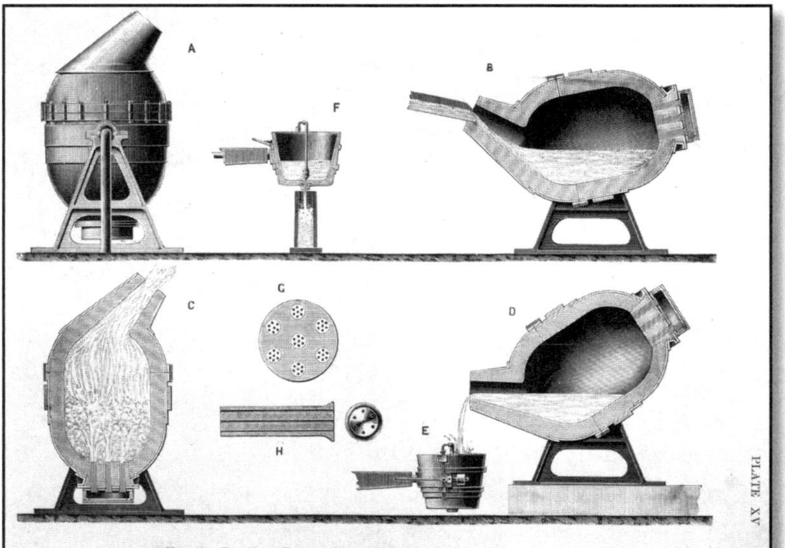

Fig. 43. The First Form of Bessemer Moveable Converter and Ladle

The introduction of the Bessemer converter, diagrammed above, revolutionized steel production and represented one of many technological milestones in the second half of the 19th century. SSPL via Getty Images

and for processes such as cream separation in the dairy industry. In factories themselves, a new round of innovation by the 1890s brought larger looms to the textile industry and automatic processes to shoe manufacture and machine- and shipbuilding (through automatic riveters) that reduced skill requirements and greatly increased per capita production. Technological transformation was virtually universal in industrial societies. Work speeded up still further, semiskilled operatives became increasingly characteristic, and, on the plus side, production and thus prosperity reached new heights.

Organizational changes matched the "second industrial revolution" in technology. More expensive equipment, plus economies made possible by increasing scale, promoted the formation of larger businesses. All western European countries eased limits on the formation of joint-stock corporations from the 1850s, and the rate of corporate growth was breathtaking by the end of the century. Giant corporations grouped together to influence the terms of trade, especially in countries such as Germany, where cartels controlled as much as 90 percent of production in the electrical equipment and chemical industries. Big business techniques had a direct impact on labour. Increasingly, engineers set production quotas, displacing not only individual workers but also foremen, by introducing time-and-motion procedures designed to maximize efficiency.

Modifications in Social Structure

Developments in technology and organization reshaped social structure. A recognizable peasantry continued to exist in western Europe, but it increasingly had to adapt to new methods. In many areas (most notably, the Netherlands and Denmark) a cooperative movement spread to allow peasants to market dairy goods and other specialties to the growing urban areas without abandoning individual landownership. Many peasants began to achieve new levels of education and to adopt innovations such as new crops, better seeds, and fertilizers. They also began to innovate politically, learning to press governments to protect their agricultural interests.

In the cities the working classes continued to expand, and distinctions between artisans and factory workers, though real, began to fade. A new urban class emerged as sales outlets proliferated and growing managerial bureaucracies (both private and public) created the need for secretaries, bank tellers, and other clerical workers. A lower middle class, composed of salaried personnel who could boast a certain level of education—indeed, whose jobs depended on literacy—and who worked in conditions different from manufacturing labourers, added an important ingredient to European society and politics. Though their material conditions differed little from those of some factory workers, and though they, too, were subject to bosses and to challenging new technologies such as typewriters and cash registers, most white-collar workers shunned association with blue-collar ranks. Big business employers encouraged this separation by setting up separate payment systems and benefit programs, for they were eager to avoid a union of interests that might augment labour unrest.

At the top of European society a new upper class formed as big business took shape, representing a partial amalgam of aristocratic landowners and corporate magnates. This upper class wielded immense political influence, for example, in supporting government armaments buildups that provided markets for heavy industrial goods and jobs for aristocratic military officers.

Along with modifications in social structure came important shifts in popular behaviour, some of them cutting across class lines. As a result of growing production, prosperity increased throughout most of western Europe. Major economic recessions interrupted this prosperity, as factory output could outstrip demand and as investment speculation could, relatedly, outstrip real economic gains. Speculative bank crises and economic downturns occurred in the mid-1850s and particularly in the middle years of both the 1870s and '90s, causing substantial hardship and even wider uncertainty. Nevertheless, the general trend in standards of living for most groups was upward, allowing ordinary people to improve their diets and housing and maintain a small margin for additional purchases. The success of mass newspapers, for example, which reached several million subscribers by the 1890s, depended on the ability to pay as well as on literacy. A bicycle craze, beginning among the middle classes in the 1880s and gradually spreading downward, represented a consumer passion for a more expensive item. Improvement in standards of living was aided by a general reduction in the birth rate, which developed rapidly among urban workers and even peasants. Families increasingly regarded children as an expense, to be weighed against other possibilities, and altered traditional behaviour accordingly. Reduction in the birth rate was achieved in part by sexual abstinence but also by the use of birth control devices, which had been widely available since the vulcanization of rubber in the 1840s, and by illegal abortions, while infanticide continued in rural areas. Completing the installation of a new demographic regime was a rapid decline in infant mortality after 1880.

Rising living standards were accompanied by increased leisure time. Workers pressed for a workday of 12, then 10

Changing economic conditions throughout western Europe in the late 19th century permitted increased leisure time and the emergence of new consumer interests, such as cycling. Three Lions/Hulton Archive/ Getty Images

hours, and shortly after 1900 a few groups began to demand an even shorter period. Scattered vacation days also were introduced, and the "English weekend," which allowed time off on Saturday afternoons as well as Sundays, spread widely. Middle-class groups, for their part, loosened their previous work ethic in order to accommodate a wider range of leisure activities.

The second half of the 19th century witnessed the birth of modern leisure in western Europe and, to an extent, beyond. Team sports were played in middle-class schools and through a variety of amateur and professional teams. Many sports, such as soccer (football), had originated in traditional games but now gained standardized rules, increasing specialization among players, and the impassioned record-keeping appropriate to an industrial age. Sports commanded widespread participation among various social groups and served as the basis for extensive commercial operations. Huge stadiums and professional leagues signaled the advent of a new level of spectatorship. While many sports primarily focused on male interests, women began to participate in tennis and entire families in pastimes such as croquet and bicycling.

Leisure options were by no means confined to sports. Mass newspapers emphasized entertaining feature stories rather than politics. Parks and museums open to the public became standard urban features. Train excursions to beaches won wide patronage from factory workers as well as middle-class vacationers. A popular theatre expanded in the cities; British music halls, typical of the genre, combined song and satire, poking fun at life's tribulations and providing an escapist emphasis on pleasure-seeking. After 1900, similar themes spilled into the new visual technology that soon coalesced into early motion pictures.

The Rise of Organized Labour and Mass Protests

Mass leisure coexisted interestingly with the final major social development of the later 19th century, the escalating forms of class conflict. Pressed by the rapid pace and often dulling routine of work, antagonized by a faceless corporate management structure seemingly bent on efficiency at all costs, workers in various categories developed more active protest modes in the later 19th century. They were aided by their growing familiarity with basic industrial conditions, which facilitated the formation of relevant demands and made organization more feasible. Legal changes, spreading widely in western Europe after 1870, reduced political barriers to unionization and strikes, though clashes with government forces remained a common part of labour unrest.

Mass Leisure: The Example of the United Kingdom

Leisure emerged as a distinct concept and activity, at least on a mass scale, only when the hours of labour diminished and became more regular; before then, work and nonwork activities had been closely related to each other. In the United Kingdom in the 1850s, those who worked in textiles, the leading sector of the economy, benefitted from a regular working day and week. A half-day of leisure, Saturday, also eventually emerged. Hours of labour began to approximate nine per day in the 1870s.

As workers gained leisure time, the idea of "recreation" began to emerge—that is, nonwork time should be a time of re-creating the body and mind for the chief purpose of work. The idea grew too that this recreation should be "rational." The characteristic institutions of these new initiatives were the Mechanics Institutes for labourers and the Atheneaums for the sons—though not the daughters—of the more wealthy. Beyond these institutions there was the remarkable growth of those concerned with bringing culture to propertied urbanites, notably art galleries. However, it was not until mid-century that such initiatives began to develop rapidly, as in Manchester in the 1850s, where the Halle Orchestra was established on a professional basis and its concerts opened to anyone who could pay admission, unlike earlier, purely subscription-based music organizations. In the same decade, Owens College, the forerunner of the University of Manchester, was founded. The development of these institutions marked the emergence of a more self-consciously public middle-class culture, one remodelled around a more open and inclusive notion of what public life involved.

In terms of popular culture, a more regularized and less demanding working day and week became part of a new kind of working year, so that old calendrical observances and rituals were lost. At the same time, a number were retained, being transformed to serve new purposes in the changed circumstances of increasing urbanization and industrialization. For instance, the old, established local "feast" and "wake" days of the industrial districts in the north of England were retained, serving many of the old communal functions yet also changing character and obtaining new functions in light of the spread of the railway and the advent of the modern vacation. Communal identities might now be formed by leaving the towns en masse, either for the railway excursion or on holiday, when large sections of the workers from particular towns took their leisure together at the new seaside resorts such as Blackpool. In urban Britain, restrictions upon space as well as upon time shaped the new culture, with old places of congregation, such as common lands on which fairs had been held, now being built over as towns grew. In the process, leisure often moved indoors, becoming more regular and more commercial in its organization. Commercial pressures in fact were most responsible for reshaping what had at least from the late 18th century been identified as popular culture, as opposed to forms of high culture. (Institutions such as the new urban concert halls of the mid-19th century were important in fostering a notion of the sublime and sacral nature of classical music, in contrast to the "low" music of the other sort of urban concert hall, namely the music hall.)

Commercialization of public culture was evident in the music hall from the 1850s, though more so in the late 19th century, with the construction of large purpose-built halls and the development of a nationwide chain of venues and a national "star" system. Before then, even if commercial, organizations were smaller-scale, less commercial, and more locally rooted. Commercial pressures were accompanied by political and moral pressures from above. The civic provision of culture was intended not only for the well-to-do but also for the mass of the population. For example, the public park, from its introduction in the 1840s, was an attempt to reproduce rational recreation among the lower classes through the design of the park as a place where civilized and rational behaviour and deportment could be encouraged. Of course, in practice, parks served other purposes, but their place in what was a widespread and marked reshaping of popular manners should not be underestimated. Commercial and reform interests also combined in the proliferation of reading matter for the "popular classes." Indeed, the creation of a literate population was one of the most striking achievements of the century.

Not surprisingly, given the mood of reaction following the failures of the 1848 revolutions, the 1850s constituted a period of relative placidity in labour relations. Skilled workers in Britain formed a conservative craft union movement, known as New Model Unionism, that urged calm negotiation and respectability; a number of durable trade unions were formed as a result, and a minority of workers gained experience in national organization. Miners and factory workers rose in strikes occasionally, signaling a class-based tension with management in many areas, but no consistent pattern developed.

The depression of the 1870s, which brought new hardship and reminded workers of the uncertainty of their lot, encouraged a wider range of agitation, and by the 1890s mass unionism surfaced throughout western Europe. Not only artisans but also factory workers and relatively unskilled groups, such as dockers, showed a growing ability to form national unions that made use of the sheer power of numbers, even in default of special skills, to press for gains. Strike rates increased steadily. In 1892 French workers struck 261 times against 500 companies; most of the efforts remained small and local, and only 50,000 workers were involved. By 1906, the peak French strike year before 1914, 1,309 strikes brought 438,000 workers off the job. British and German strike rates were higher still; in Britain, more than 2,000,000 workers struck between 1909 and 1913. A number of nationwide strikes showed labour's new muscle.

Unionization formed the second prong of the new labour surge. Along with mass unions in individual industries, general federations formed at the national level, such as the British Trades Union Congress and the French and Italian general confederations of labour. Unions provided social and material benefits for members along with their protest action. In many industries they managed to win collective bargaining procedures with employers, though this was far from a uniform pattern in an atmosphere of bitter competition over management rights. Unions also could influence governmental decisions in the labour area.

The rise of organized labour signaled an unprecedented development in the history of European popular protest. Never before had so many people been formally organized; never before had withdrawal of labour served as the chief protest weapon. Many workers joined a sweeping ideological fervor to their protest. Many were socialists, and a number of trade union movements were tightly linked to the rising socialist parties. This was particularly true in Germany and Austria. In other areas, especially France and Italy, an alternative syndicalist ideology won many adherents in the union movement; syndicalists urged that direct action through strikes should topple governments and usher in a new age in which organizations of workers would control production. Against these varied revolutionary currents, many workers saw in unions and strikes primarily a means to compensate for changes in their work environment, through higher pay (as a reward for less pleasant labour) and shorter hours. Even here, there was an ability to seek new ends rather than appealing to past standards. Overall, pragmatism battled with ideology in most labour movements, and in point of fact none of the large organizations aimed primarily at revolution.

Labour unrest was not the only form of protest in the later 19th century. In many continental nations (but not in Britain or Scandinavia), nationalist organizations drew the attention of discontented shopkeepers and others in the lower middle class who felt pressed by new business forms, such as department stores and elaborate managerial bureaucracies, but who were also hostile to socialism and the union movement. Nationalist riots surfaced periodically in many countries around such issues as setbacks in imperialist competition or internal political scandals. Some of the riots and accompanying organizations were also anti-Semitic, holding Jews responsible for big business and socialism alike. France witnessed the most important agitation from the radical right, through organizations like the Action Française, but anti-Semitic political movements also developed in Germany and Austria.

Important women's movements completed the new roster of mass protests. The basic conditions of women did not change greatly in western Europe during the second half of the 19th century, with the significant exception of the rapidly declining birth rate. The steady spread of primary education increased female literacy, bringing it nearly equal to male levels by 1900. A growing minority of middle-class women also entered secondary schools, and by the 1870s a handful reached universities and professional schools. Several separate women's colleges were founded in centres such as Oxford and Cambridge, and, against heavy resistance, a few women became doctors and lawyers. For somewhat larger numbers of women, new jobs in the service sector of the economy, such as telephone operators, primary-school teachers, and nurses, provided opportunities for work before marriage. Gradually some older sectors of employment, such as domestic service, began to decline. Nevertheless, emphasis on a domestic sphere for women changed little. Public schools, while teaching literacy, also taught the importance of household skills and support for a working husband.

These were the circumstances that produced increasingly active feminist movements, sometimes independently and sometimes in association with socialist parties. Feminist leaders sought greater equality under the law, an attack on a double-standard sexuality that advantaged men. Above all, they came to concentrate on winning the vote. Massive petitions in Britain, accompanied by considerable violence after 1900, signaled Europe's most active feminist movement, drawing mainly on middle-class ranks. Feminists in Scandinavia were successful in winning voting rights after 1900. Almost everywhere, feminist pressures added to the new variety of mass protest action.

Conditions in Eastern Europe

Social conditions in eastern and southern Europe differed substantially from those of the west, but there were some common elements. Middle- and upper-class women in Russia, for example, surged into new educational and professional opportunities in some numbers. Growing cities and factories produced some trade union activity, on the part of skilled groups such as the printers and metalworkers, that resembled efforts elsewhere.

Rural conditions, however, were vastly different from those in western Europe. Eastern and southern Europe remained dominated by the peasantry, as urbanization, though rapid, was at a far earlier stage. Peasant conditions were generally poor. Amid growing population pressure, many peasants suffered from a lack of land in areas dominated by large estates. One result was rapid emigration, to the Americas and elsewhere, from Spain, southern Italy, and eastern Europe. Another result was recurrent unrest. Peasants in southern Spain, loosely organized under anarchist banners, rose almost once a decade in the late 19th century, seizing land and burning estate records.

The social and economic situation was most complex in Russia. Stung by the loss of the Crimean War (1854–56) to Britain, France, and the Ottoman Empire, literally in their own backyard, Russian leaders decided on a modernization program. The key ingredient was an end to the rigid manorial system, and in 1861 Alexander II, a reform-minded tsar, issued the Emancipation Manifesto, freeing the serfs. This act sought to produce a freer labour market but also to protect the status of the nobility. As a result, noble landlords retained some of the best land and were paid for the loss of their servile labour. In turn, serfs, though technically in control of most land, owed redemption payments to the state. This arrangement produced important changes in the countryside. Peasants did develop some commercial habits, aided by gradually spreading education and literacy. More and more peasants migrated, temporarily or permanently, to cities, where they swelled the manufacturing labour force and also the ranks of urban poor. Rural unrest continued, however, as peasants resented their taxes and payments and the large estates that remained.

From the 1870s the Russian government also launched a program of industrial development, beginning with the construction of a national rail network capped by the Trans-Siberian Railroad. Factory industry was encouraged; much of it was held under foreign ownership, though a native entrepreneurial class emerged. Large factories developed to produce textiles and to process metals. Conditions remained poor, however, and combined with the unfamiliar pace of factory work and rural grievances to spur recurrent worker unrest. Illegal strikes and unions became increasingly prominent after 1900. A minority of urban workers, especially in St. Petersburg and Moscow, were won to socialist doctrines, and a well-organized Marxist movement arose, its leadership after 1900 increasingly dominated by Vladimir Ilich Lenin, a creative theorist who adapted Marxist theory to the Russian situation and who concentrated single-mindedly on creating the network of underground cells that could foment outright revolution. Russia was embarked on a genuine industrial revolution. With its massive size and resources, it ranked among world leaders in many categories of production by 1900. However, it operated in an exceptionally unstable social and political climate.

THE EMERGENCE OF THE INDUSTRIAL STATE

During the second half of the 19th century, politics and socioeconomic conditions became increasingly intertwined in Europe, producing a new definition of government functions, including a greatly expanded state and a new political spectrum. Linkage to cultural trends also showed through an interest in hard-headed realism. Predictably, political conditions in eastern Europe, though mirroring some of the general developments, remained distinctive.

Political Patterns

The decades between 1850 and 1870 served as a crucial turning point in European politics and diplomacy, somewhat surprisingly given the apparent victory of conservative forces over the revolutions of 1848. Reactionary impulses did surface during these years. A Conservative Party eager to hold the line against further change emerged in Prussia. A number of governments made new arrangements with the Roman Catholic Church to encourage religion against political attacks. Pope Pius IX, who had been chased from Rome during the final surge of agitation in 1848, turned adamantly against new political ideas. In the *Syllabus of Errors* accompanying the encyclical *Quanta cura* ("With What Great Care," 1864), he denounced liberalism and nationalism and insisted on the duty of Roman Catholic rulers to protect the established church, even against religious toleration. The proclamation of papal

Conservative British politician Benjamin Disraeli, who twice served as Britain's prime minister (1868, 1874–80). Jabez Hughes/Hulton Archive/Getty Images

infallibility (1870) was widely seen as another move to firm up church authority against change.

Many conservative leaders, however, saw the victory over revolution as a chance to innovate within the framework of the established order. They were aided by a pragmatic current among liberals, many of whom were convinced that compromise, not revolution, was the only way to win reform. Thus, in Britain Benjamin Disraeli, the Conservative leader in the House of Commons, in 1867 sponsored a new suffrage measure, which granted the vote to most urban workers. Disraeli hoped that the new voters would support his party, and some of them did so. In France Emperor Napoleon III, who had insisted on an authoritarian regime during the 1850s, began to sponsor major industrial development while maintaining an active foreign policy, designed to win growing support for the state. In the 1860s, pressed by diplomatic setbacks,

Napoleon also granted liberal concessions, expanding parliamentary power and tolerating more freedom of press and speech. The Habsburg monarchy promoted an efficient, largely German bureaucracy to replace the defunct manorial regime and in the 1860s sought to make peace with the leading nationalist movement. In the *Ausgleich* ("compromise") of 1867, Hungary was granted substantial autonomy, and separate parliaments, though based on limited suffrage, were established in Austria and Hungary. This result enraged Slavic nationalists, but it signaled an important departure from previous policies bent on holding the line against any dilution of imperial power.

The key centres of dynamic conservatism, however, were Italy and Germany. In the Italian state of Piedmont during the early 1850s, the able prime minister, Camillo di Cavour, conciliated liberals by sponsoring economic development and granting new personal freedoms. Cavour worked especially to capture the current of Italian nationalism. By a series of diplomatic maneuvers, he won an alliance with France against Austria and, in a war fought in 1859, drove Austria from the province of Lombardy. Nationalist risings followed elsewhere in Italy, and Cavour was able to join these to a new Italian state under the Piedmontese king. The resultant new state had a parliament, and it vigorously attacked the power of the Roman Catholic Church in a liberal-nationalist combination that could win support from various political groups.

Inspired in part by Italian example, a young chief minister in Prussia, Otto von Bismarck, began a still more important campaign of limited political reform and nationalist aggrandizement. The goal was to unite Germany under Prussia and to defuse liberal and radical agitation. In a series of carefully calculated wars during the 1860s, Bismarck first defeated Denmark and won control over German-speaking provinces. He then provoked

Otto von Bismarck, Prussian prime minister and founder and first chancellor of the German Empire. Hulton Archive/Getty Images

Austria, Prussia's chief rival in Germany, and to general surprise won handily, relying on Prussia's well-organized military might. A Prussian-dominated union of northern German states was formed. A final war with France, in 1870–71, again resulted in Prussian victory. This time the prize was the province of Alsace and part of Lorraine and agreement with the southern German states to form a single German empire under the Prussian ruler. This new state had a national parliament with a lower house based on universal manhood suffrage but an upper house dominated by Prussia, whose own parliament was elected by a voting system that assured the political power of the wealthiest elements of society. As in Italy, appointment of ministers lay with the crown, not parliament. Freedoms of press and speech were extended and religious liberty expanded to include Jews, but the government periodically intervened against dissident political groups.

These developments radically changed Europe's map, eliminating two traditional vacuums of power that had been dominated by a welter of smaller states. Nationalism was triumphant in central Europe. At the same time, regimes had been created that, buoyed by nationalist success, appealed to moderate liberal and conservative elements alike while fully contenting neither group. The old regime, attacked for so many decades, was gone, as parliamentary politics and a party system predominated through western and central Europe. Concurrently, important powers for throne and aristocracy remained, as liberals either compromised their policies or went into sullen, usually ineffective, opposition.

A slightly different version of the politics of compromise emerged in France in the 1870s. Defeated by Prussia, the empire of Napoleon III collapsed. A variety of political forces, including various monarchist groups, contended for succession after a radical rising, the Paris

Commune, failed in 1871. Eventually, through a piecemeal series of laws, conservative republicans triumphed, winning a parliamentary majority through elections and proclaiming the Third Republic. This was a clearly liberal regime, in which parliament dominated the executive branch amid frequent changes of ministry. Freedoms of press, speech, and association were widely upheld, and the regime attacked the powers of the church in education and other areas. At the same time, dominant liberals pledged to avoid significant social change, winning peasant and middle-class support on this basis.

With the emergence of the Third Republic, the constitutional structure of western Europe was largely set for the remainder of the 19th century. All the major nations (except Spain, which continued to oscillate between periods of liberalism and conservative authoritarianism) had parliaments and a multiparty system, and most had granted universal manhood suffrage. Britain completed this process by a final electoral reform in the mid-1880s. Belgium, Italy, and Austria held out for a longer time, experiencing considerable popular unrest as a result, though voting reforms for men were completed before 1914. Important political crises still surfaced. Bismarck warred with the Roman Catholic Church and the Catholic Centre Party during the 1870s before reaching a compromise agreement. He then tried virtually to outlaw the socialist party, which remained on the defensive until a liberalization after he fell from power in 1890. During the 1890s, France faced a major constitutional crisis in the Dreyfus affair. The imprisonment of Alfred Dreyfus, a Jewish army officer falsely accused of treason, triggered a battle between conservative, Catholic, and military forces, all bent on defending the authority of army and state, and a more radical republican group joined by socialists, who saw the future of the republic at stake. The winning pro-Dreyfus

Alfred Dreyfus, a Jewish French army officer falsely accused of treason and placed at the centre of a 12-year-long political crisis concerning his innocence, was imprisoned on Devils Island between 1895 and 1899. Hulton Archive/Getty Images

forces forced the separation of church and state by 1905, reducing Catholicism's claims on the French government and limiting the role of religion as a political issue.

The politics of compromise also affected organized religion, partly because of attacks from various states. A number of Protestant leaders took up social issues,

Dreyfus Affair

The Dreyfus affair was a political crisis, beginning in 1894 and continuing through 1906, in France during the Third Republic. The controversy centred on the question of the guilt or innocence of army captain Alfred Dreyfus, who had been convicted of treason for allegedly selling military secrets to the Germans in December 1894. At first the public supported the conviction; it was willing to believe in the guilt of Dreyfus, who was Jewish. Much of the early publicity surrounding the case came from anti-Semitic groups (especially the newspaper *La Libre Parole*, edited by Édouard Drumont), to whom Dreyfus symbolized the supposed disloyalty of French Jews.

The effort to reverse the sentence was at first limited to members of the Dreyfus family, but, as evidence pointing to the guilt of another French officer, Ferdinand Walsin-Esterhazy, came to light from 1896, the pro-Dreyfus side slowly gained adherents (among them journalists Joseph Reinach and Georges Clemenceau—the future World War I premier—and a senator, Auguste Scheurer-Kestner). The accusations against Esterhazy resulted in a court-martial that acquitted him of treason (January 1898). To protest against the verdict, the novelist Émile Zola wrote a letter titled "J'accuse," published in Clemenceau's newspaper *L'Aurore*. In it he attacked the army for covering up its mistaken conviction of Dreyfus, an action for which Zola was found guilty of libel.

By the time of the Zola letter, the Dreyfus case had attracted widespread public attention and had split France into two opposing camps. The anti-Dreyfusards (those against reopening the case) viewed the controversy as an attempt by the nation's enemies to discredit the army and weaken France. The Dreyfusards (those seeking exoneration of Captain Dreyfus) saw the issue as the principle of the freedom of the individual subordinated to that of national security. They wanted to republicanize the army and put it under parliamentary control.

From 1898 to 1899 the Dreyfusard cause gained in strength. In August 1898 an important document implicating Dreyfus was found to be a forgery. After Maj. Hubert-Joseph Henry of the intelligence section confessed to fabricating the document in order to strengthen the army's position, revision was made almost certain. At the same time, the affair was becoming a question of vital concern to politicians. The republican parties in the Chamber of Deputies recognized that the increasingly vocal nationalist right posed a threat to the parliamentary regime. Led by the Radicals, a left-wing coalition was formed. In response to continuing disorders and demonstrations, a cabinet headed by the Radical René Waldeck-Rousseau was set up in June 1899 with the express purpose of defending the republic and with the hope of settling the judicial side of the Dreyfus case as soon as possible. When a new court-martial, held at Rennes, found Dreyfus guilty in September 1899, the president of the republic, in order to resolve the issue, pardoned him. In July 1906 a civilian court of appeals (the Cour d'Appel) set aside the judgment of the Rennes court and rehabilitated Dreyfus. The army, however, did not publicly declare his innocence until 1995.

With the Dreyfusards in the ascendant, the affair marked the start of a new phase in the history of the Third Republic, a phase in which a series of Radical-led governments pursued an anticlerical policy that culminated in the formal separation of church and state (1905). By intensifying antagonisms between right and left and by forcing individuals to choose sides, the case made a lasting impact on the consciousness of the French nation.

seeking new ways to reach the urban poor and to alleviate distress. The Salvation Army, founded in Britain in 1878, expressed the social mission idea, whereby practical measures were used in the service of God. Under a new pope, Leo XIII, the Roman Catholic Church moved more formally to accommodate to modern politics. The encyclical *Rerum Novarum* ("Of New Things," 1891) urged Catholics to accept political institutions such as parliaments and universal suffrage. It proclaimed sympathy for working people against the excesses of capitalism, justifying moderate trade union action though vigorously denouncing socialism. Steps such as this muted religious issues in politics, while on the whole relegating organized religion to a more modest public role.

In general, the resolution of major constitutional issues led to an alternation of moderate conservative and liberal forces in power between 1870 and 1914. Conservatives, when in charge, tended to push a more openly nationalistic foreign policy than did liberals. Liberals, as the Dreyfus affair suggested in France, tended to be more concerned about limiting the role of religion in political life. Both movements, however, agreed on many basic goals, including political structure itself. Both were capable of promoting some modest social reforms, though neither wished to go too far. In Italy, conservatives and liberals were so similar that commentators noted a process of transformism (*trasformismo*), by which parliamentary deputies, regardless of their electoral platforms, were transformed into virtually identical power seekers once in Rome.

As the range of dispute between conservatives and liberals narrowed (save for fringe movements of the radical right that distrusted parliamentary politics altogether), the most striking innovation in the political spectrum was the rise of socialist parties, based primarily on working-class support though with scattered rural and middle-class backing as well. Formal socialist parties began to take shape in the 1860s. They differed from previous socialist movements in focusing primarily on winning electoral support; earlier socialist leaders either had been openly revolutionary or had favoured setting up model communities that, they thought, would produce change through example. Most of the socialist parties established in the 1860s and '70s derived their inspiration from Karl Marx. They argued that revolution was essential and that capitalists and workers were locked in a historic battle that must affect all social institutions. The goal of socialist action was to seize the state, establishing proletarian control and unseating the exploitative powers of capitalism. In practice, however, most socialist parties worked through the political process (with support for trade union activities), diluting orthodox Marxism. Universal manhood suffrage created a climate ripe for socialist gains, especially since, in most countries, these parties were the first to realize the nature of mass politics. They set up permanent organizations to woo support even apart from election campaigns and sponsored impassioned political rallies rather than working behind the scenes to manipulate voters. Newspapers, educational efforts, and social activities supplemented the formal political message.

By the 1880s the German socialist party was clearly winning working-class support away from the liberal movement despite Bismarck's antisocialist laws. By 1900 the party was a major political force, gaining about two million votes in key elections and seating a large minority of parliamentary deputies. By 1913 the German party was polling four million votes in national elections and was the largest single political force in the nation. Socialist parties in Austria, Scandinavia, and the Low Countries won similar success. Socialism in France and Italy, divided among various ideological factions, was somewhat slower to coalesce, but it too gained ground steadily. In 1899 a socialist entered the French Cabinet as part of the Dreyfusard coalition, shocking orthodox Marxists who argued against collaboration with bourgeois politicians. By 1913 the French party had more than a hundred delegates in parliament. British socialism grew later and with less attention to formal ideology. The Labour Party was formed in the 1890s with strong trade union connections; it long lagged behind the Liberals in winning workers' votes. Nevertheless, even in Britain the party was a strong third force by 1914. In many countries socialists not only formed a large national minority capable of pressing government coalitions but also won control of many municipal governments, where they increased welfare benefits and regulated urban conditions for the benefit of their constituents.

The rise of socialism put what was called "the social question" at the forefront of domestic policy in the late 19th century, replacing debates about formal constitutional structure. Fear of socialism strengthened the hand of ruling conservative or liberal coalitions. At the same time, success mellowed many socialist leaders. In Germany about 1900 a revisionist movement arose that judged that revolution was not necessary. It was thought that Marxism should be modified to allow for piecemeal political gains and cooperation with middle-class reformers. Most parties officially denounced revisionism in favour of stricter Marxism, but in fact they behaved in a revisionist fashion.

Changes in Government Functions

Shifts in the political spectrum and larger issues of industrial society prompted important changes in government functions through the second half of the 19th century. Mass education headed the list. Building on earlier precedents, most governments in western Europe established universal public schooling in the 1870s and '80s, requiring attendance at least at the primary levels. Education was seen as essential to provide basic skills such as literacy and numeracy. It also was a vital means of conditioning citizens to loyalty to the national government. All the educational systems vigorously pushed nationalism in their history and literature courses. They tried to standardize language, as against minority dialects and languages (opposing Polish in Germany, for example, or Breton in France).

A second extension of government functions involved peacetime military conscription, which was resisted only in Great Britain. Prussia's success in war during the 1860s convinced other continental powers that military service was essential, and conscription, along with steadily growing armaments expenditures, enhanced the military readiness of most governments.

Governments also expanded their record-keeping functions, replacing church officials. Requirements for civil marriages (in addition to religious ceremonies where desired), census-taking, and other activities steadily expanded state impact in these areas. Regulatory efforts increased from the 1850s. Central governments inspected food-processing facilities and housing. Inspectors checked to make sure that safety provisions and rules on work hours and the employment of women and children were observed. Other functionaries carefully patrolled borders, requiring passports for entry. Most countries (Britain again was an exception) increased tariff regulations in the 1890s, seeking to conciliate agriculturalists and industrialists alike; while not a new function, this signaled the state's activist role in basic economic policy. Most European governments ran all or part of the railroad system and set up telephone services as part of postal operations.

Educator, record-keeper, military recruiter, major economic actor—the state also entered the welfare field during the 1880s. Bismarck pioneered with three social insurance laws between 1883 and 1889—part of his abortive effort to beat down socialism—that set up rudimentary schemes for protection in illness, accident, and old age. Austria and Scandinavia imitated the German system, while the French and Italian governments established somewhat more voluntary programs. Britain enacted a major welfare insurance scheme under a Liberal administration in 1906, and in 1911 it became the first country to institute state-run unemployment insurance. All these measures were limited in scope, providing modest benefits at best, but they marked the beginnings of a full-fledged welfare state.

The growth of government, and the explosion of its range of services, was reflected in the rapid expansion of state bureaucracies. Most countries installed formal civil service procedures by the 1870s, with examinations designed to assure employment and seniority by merit rather than favouritism. State-run secondary schools, designed to train aspiring bureaucrats, slowly increased their output of graduates. Taxation increased as well, and just before the outbreak of war in 1914, several nations installed income tax provisions to provide additional revenue. Quietly, amid many national variants, a new kind of state was constructed during the late 19th century, with far more elaborate and intimate contacts with the citizenry than ever before in European history.

Reform and Reaction in Eastern Europe

Political patterns in Spain, the smaller nations of southeastern Europe, and, above all, Russia followed a rather different rhythm. Parliamentary institutions were installed in some cases after 1900, but these were carefully controlled. Censorship severely limited political expression.

Russia continued a reformist mode for several years after the emancipation of the serfs. New local governments were created to replace manorial rule, and local assemblies helped regulate their activities, giving outlet for political expression to many professional people who served these governments as doctors, teachers, and jurists. Law codes were standardized and punishments lightened. The military was reformed and became an important force in providing basic education to conscripts. No national representative body existed, however, as tsarist authority was maintained. Further, after Alexander II's assassination by anarchists in 1881, the government reversed its reformist tendencies. Police powers expanded. Official campaigns lashed out brutally at Jews and other national minorities. Agitation continued at various levels, among intellectuals (many of whom were anarchists) and among workers and peasants. A small liberal current took shape within the expanding middle class as well.

Economic recession early in the 1900s was followed by a shocking loss in a war with Japan (1904–05). These conditions led to outright revolution in 1905, as worker strikes and peasant rioting spread through the country. Nicholas II responded with a number of concessions. Redemption payments were eased on peasants, and enterprising farmers gained new rights to acquire land, creating a successful though widely resented kulak class in the countryside. Rural unrest eased as a result. On the political front a national parliament, or Duma, was established. Socialist candidates, however, were not allowed to run, and the Duma soon became a mere rubber stamp, unable to take any significant initiative. Repression returned and with it substantial popular unrest, including growing illegal trade unions. Russia did not make the turn to compromise politics, and in the judgment of some historians renewed revolution loomed even aside from the outbreak of war in 1914.

Diplomatic Entanglements

Many features of Europe's evolution in the late 19th century turned renewed attention to the diplomatic and military arena. Advancing industrialization heightened competition among individual nations and created a massive power disparity between Europe and most of the rest of the world. Wealth allowed new international ventures. Specific inventions such as steamships (capable of rapid oceanic transit and travel upstream in such previously unnavigable waters as the rivers of Africa), machine guns, and new medicines provided fresh opportunities for world domination. The changes in Europe's map caused by Italian and German unification inevitably prompted diplomatic reshufflings. The politics of compromise encouraged governments to rely on diplomatic goals as a means of pleasing the new and somewhat unpredictable electorate.

During the 1870s and '80s Europe itself remained relatively calm. Bismarck, by far the ablest statesman on the scene, professed the newly united Germany to be a satisfied power, interested only in maintaining the European status quo. His most obvious opponent was recently defeated France, and he carefully constructed a diplomatic network that would make French enmity impotent. Peacetime alliances were an innovation in European diplomacy, but for a time they had the desired stabilizing effect. Bismarck conciliated the Habsburg regime, forming an arrangement in 1879 between the two emperors. In 1882 he joined Italy to this understanding, completing a Triple Alliance on the basis of assurances of mutual aid against outside attack. Beyond this, Bismarck negotiated a separate understanding with Russia in 1887. These linkages required sensitive juggling, because they loosely grouped some potential opponents (such as Russia and the Habsburgs). They did offer a means of isolating France, especially since Bismarck also cultivated good relations with Britain, which was interested primarily in colonial expansion where France was its most obvious rival.

Even before it was fully constructed, Bismarck's plan to stabilize Europe faced an important challenge. Revolts in the Balkans, in areas nominally under Ottoman control, called attention to what was then Europe's most volatile area. Effective Ottoman dominion over this region had been declining steadily along with the vigour of the government more generally, and nationalist fervor, spreading from western Europe, had galvanized many ethnic groups. Revolts in Serbia and Romania won partial independence earlier in the 19th century, and Greece had gained national status outright. In the 1870s rioting broke out in several regions, and Serbia and another small nation, Montenegro, declared war on the Ottoman empire. Russia joined in, to protect its Slavic "brethren" and to gain new territory at Turkey's expense. Easy victories followed, and a large new Bulgarian state was proclaimed, along with Russian acquisitions along the Black Sea. At this point Austria-Hungary and Britain, both interested in stability in the region, intervened. Bismarck, anxious for peace, called a Berlin Congress in 1878 to win an acceptable compromise. The result was a smaller Bulgaria, full independence for Serbia, Montenegro, and Romania, and Austrian occupation of the Slavic provinces of Bosnia and Herzegovina. Britain gained the island of Cyprus, which gave it a closer watchdog position over its routes to India, and France was encouraged to take over Tunisia. The great loser at the Congress of Berlin was Russia, which left resentful that its enormous gains were nullified. Although Bismarck claimed that Germany had acted as an honest broker, the Russians believed that he had favoured Austria-Hungary. Germany would not be able to conciliate Russia for almost a decade. In the meantime, Bismarck's alliance system unfolded in the wake of the Congress of Berlin with Germany siding first with Austria-Hungary because both countries faced Russian enmity.

The Scramble for Colonies

The most obvious result of the Congress and of nationalist yearnings, juxtaposed with a more structured European map, was a new and general scramble for colonies in other parts of the world. Even before the 1870s some new gains had occurred. French explorers fanned out in equatorial Africa, and a French mission began the conquest of Indochina in the 1860s. Many European nations exhibited a growing interest in colonies as sources of raw materials and new markets and as potential outlets for excess population and for administrators who could not be accommodated at home. Opportunities for individual adventurism and profit also ran high. Overriding motivations for the climactic imperialist scramble involved a desire to appeal to domestic nationalism and an interest in maintaining or gaining place as world powers. New nations such as Italy and Germany sought empires to prove their status; France sought expansion to compensate for its humiliating defeat at Germany's hands; Britain pressed outward in order to protect existing colonies. Russia, and at the century's end the United States and Japan, also joined the competition.

Between 1880 and 1900 much of Asia was divided. Britain held Burma; Britain, Germany, France, and the United States divided the Pacific islands of Polynesia. All the major European powers save Italy took advantage of China's weakness to acquire long-term leases on port cities and surrounding regions, easily putting down the Chinese Boxer Rebellion against Western encroachments in 1899–1900. Germany gained new advisory and investment roles within the Ottoman Empire, while Britain and Russia divided spheres of influence in Afghanistan; Britain also effectively controlled several small states on the Persian Gulf.

The dismemberment of Africa was even more complete. Portugal expanded its control over Angola and Mozambique, Belgium took over the giant Congo region, and Germany gained new colonies in southern Africa.

Britain and France, the big winners, gained new territory in West Africa, and Britain built a network of colonies in East Africa running from South Africa to Egypt. The French occupation of Morocco and the Italian conquest of Tripoli, after 1900, completed the process. Only Ethiopia remained fully free, defeating an Italian force in 1896.

Prewar Diplomacy

By the early years of the 20th century the major imperialist gains had been completed, but some of the excitement that the process had generated remained, to spill back into European diplomacy. Germany had begun construction of a large navy, for example, in the late 1890s, in part to assure its place as an imperialist power, but this development, along with Germany's rapid industrial surge, threatened Britain. France ran a massive empire, but its nationalistic yearnings were not fully satisfied and the humiliating loss of Alsace-Lorraine had not been avenged. Russia encountered a new opponent in the Far East in the rise of Japan. The Japanese, fearful of Russian expansion in northern China, defeated the tsarist forces in the Russo-Japanese War in 1904–05, winning Korea in the process. The unstable Russian regime looked for compensatory gains in the hothouse of the Balkans rather than in the distant reaches of Asia. The stage was set for intensification of European conflicts.

Furthermore, the complex alliance system developed by Bismarck came unraveled following the statesman's removal from power in 1890 at the hands of a new emperor, William II. Germany did not renew its alliance with Russia, and during the 1890s an alliance developed between Russia and France, both fearful of Germany's might. Britain, also wary of German power, swallowed its traditional enmity and colonial rivalries with France, forming a loose Entente Cordiale in 1904; Russia joined this understanding in 1907. Europe stood divided between two alliance systems.

In 1908 Austria-Hungary annexed Bosnia and Herzegovina. It was eager to strike a blow against South Slavic nationalism, which threatened the multinational Habsburg empire. This move antagonized Russia and Serbia, the latter claiming these territories as part of its own national domain. In 1912 Russia aided several of the Balkan states in a new attack on the Ottoman Empire, with the allies hoping to obtain Macedonia. The Balkan nations won, but they quarreled with each other in the Second Balkan War in 1913. Further bitterness resulted in the Balkan region, with Serbia, though a winner in both wars, eager to take on Austria-Hungary directly.

On June 28, 1914, Gavrilo Princip, a Serbian nationalist, assassinated the Austrian Archduke and apparent heir to the throne Francis Ferdinand. Austria-Hungary resolved to crush the Serbian threat in response. Germany supported its Austrian ally, partly because it feared that its most reliable partner needed a victory and partly because many leaders judged that war had become inevitable and was preferable sooner than later, given ongoing military modernizations in France and Russia. Russia refused to abandon Serbia, and France hewed to its alliance with Russia. Last-minute negotiations, led by Britain, failed. Russia began a general mobilization following Austria's July 28 attack on Serbia. Germany, eager to take advantage of Russia's slowness by striking a lightning blow in the west, then invaded neutral Belgium and pushed into northern France. Britain, briefly hesitant, was committed by treaty to defend Belgium and entered the fray on August 4, and World War I was under way.

The patterns of European diplomacy in the late 19th century are not an unrelieved story of nationalist rivalries.

From the 1850s onward European nations signed a number of constructive international agreements designed to link postal systems, regularize principles of international commercial law, and even install some humanitarian agreements in the event of war. The International Red Cross was one fruit of these activities, as was the establishment of a World Court, in the Netherlands, to help settle international disputes. But efforts to negotiate a reduction of armaments, in a series of conferences beginning in 1899, failed completely amid growing national military buildups. Britain and Germany, in particular, refused to abandon their naval race, which took a new turn in 1906 with the development of the massive British battleship HMS *Dreadnought*.

World War I, a bloody struggle that served to reduce Europe's world role, resulted not only from escalating international tensions but also from domestic strains. Russia and Austria-Hungary, internally pressed by social and nationalist strife, looked to diplomatic successes, even at the cost of war, as a means of diverting internal discontents, and the alliance system trapped more stable nations into following suit. Germany, Britain, and France, beleaguered by growing socialist gains that frightened a conservative leadership and urged on by intense popular nationalism, also accepted war not only as a diplomatic tool but also as a means of countering internal disarray. Cultural emphasis on irrationality, spontaneity, and despair contributed to the context as well. War thus resulted from a number of basic developments in 19th-century Europe, just as its catastrophic impact resulted from the military technologies that the 19th-century industrial revolution had created.

CHAPTER 5

Modern Culture at the Turn of the 20th Century

In the last quarter of the 19th century European thought and art became prey to self-doubt and the fear, as well as the pleasures, of decadence. Writers as different as Charles Baudelaire and Matthew Arnold, Henry Adams and Gustave Flaubert, John Ruskin and Friedrich Nietzsche had begun from the mid-century onward to express their revulsion at the banality and smugness of surrounding humanity, debased—they felt—by "progress." It seemed as if with the onset of positivism and science, Realpolitik and Darwinism, realistic art and popular culture, all noble thought and true emotion had been suffocated. The only things that stood out from banality and smugness were their own appalling extremes—vulgarity and arrogance—against which all the weapons of the mind seemed powerless.

Such intellectuals and artists were hopelessly outnumbered not only in the literal sense but also in the means of influencing culture. A newspaper that reached half a million readers with its clichés, its serial story, and its garish illustrations "educated" the people in a fashion that actively prevented any understanding of high culture. The barrier was far more insurmountable than mere ignorance or illiteracy, and it was cutting off not just the populace but also—to use Arnold's terms—the barbarian upper class and the Philistine middle class. Similarly, Nietzsche anatomized what he called the culture-Philistine; that is, the person whose mind fed on middling ideas and "genteel" tastes halfway between those of the populace and those of the genuinely cultivated. Numerous artists and writers, high in repute and believed then to be the leaders of modern civilization, provided the materials for these conscientious consumers of art, literature, and "sound opinion" in every field. In other words, the prudent, self-limiting impulse of Realism after 1848 had generated the middlebrow, while the evolution of industrial democracy had generated the mass person. By the late 1880s the gap between this compact army with its honoured officers and common soldiers and the hostile, half-visible avant-garde was a permanent feature of cultural evolution.

Out of the uneven conflict came increasingly violent expressions of hatred and disgust, and the age that had defined Realism as the commonplace and average gradually succumbed to a variety of proffered opposites. Their forms and tendencies can be grouped into half a dozen kinds, not all on the same intellectual or artistic plane, nor all distinctly named then or now. One discerns first a retreat from the ugly world into a species of Neoclassicism. Such were the French poets known as Parnassians. Strict form, antique subjects, and the pose of impassivity constitute their hallmark. In painting, the work of Pierre Puvis de Chavannes stands in parallel.

In music, the explicit revolt against Richard Wagner and Franz Liszt, of which Johannes Brahms was made the torchbearer, offers similarities, particularly in the desire to learn and employ the "purer" forms of an earlier time. Likewise, the shift in tone and temper of the later poems of Alfred, Lord Tennyson, Matthew Arnold, or Théophile Gautier; the resurgence of Thomist orthodoxy (the theology of St. Thomas Aquinas) in Roman Catholic thought; the haughty detachment in the plays of Henry-François Becque and those of Henrik Ibsen's middle period, all suggest a search for stability, for a fixed point from which to judge and condemn contemporary "progress."

Decadents

The Decadent movement in literature, which emerged at the end of the 19th century in France and England, stemmed from bitter regret for the loss of a world of moral and political absolutes and from middle-class fears of supersession in a society where the power of the masses (as workers, voters, purchasers, and consumers) was slowly but inexorably on the increase. It derived from the same determinist philosophy as Naturalism and had much in common aesthetically with Impressionism in that it focused on subjectively perceived moments of physical experience, held to have no significance beyond themselves. It was also a form of late Romanticism.

Among the Decadents were the French Symbolist poets in particular and their contemporaries in England, the later generation of the Aesthetic movement. Both groups aspired to set literature and art free from the materialistic preoccupations of industrialized society, and, in both, the freedom of some members' morals helped to enlarge the connotation of the term, which is almost equivalent to *fin de siècle*.

In France it was Paul Verlaine who gladly accepted the descriptive epithet *décadent*, which had been used in a collection of parodies, *Les Déliquescences d'Adoré Floupette* (1885; "The Corruption of Adoré Floupette"), by Gabriel Vicaire and Henri Beauclair. From 1886 to 1889 appeared a review, *Le Décadent*, founded by Anatole Baju, with Verlaine among its contributors. The Decadents claimed Charles Baudelaire (d. 1867) as their inspiration and counted Arthur Rimbaud, Stéphane Mallarmé, and Tristan Corbière among themselves. Another significant figure was the novelist Joris-Karl Huysmans, who developed interest in the esoteric and whose *À rebours* (1884; *Against the Grain*) was called by Arthur Symons "the breviary of the Decadence."

In England the Decadents were 1890s figures such as Arthur Symons ("the blond angel"), Oscar Wilde, Ernest Dowson, and Lionel Johnson, who were members of the Rhymers' Club or contributors to *The Yellow Book*, an illustrated quarterly magazine devoted to aesthetics, literature, and art.

SYMBOLISM AND IMPRESSIONISM

Next, it appeared that those who wanted to withdraw from vulgar actuality were making of Art with a capital "A" an independent region of thought and feeling into which to escape, by which to reduce the pain of living. Steady contemplation of "the beautiful" created a "truer" world than the one accepted by ordinary people as real. Walter Pater, a critic writing from the shelter of Oxford, gave eloquent expression to this conception of life, in which every possible minute must be charged with fine and rare sensation. His brilliant disciple Oscar Wilde made the doctrine so clear and persuasive that it generated a characteristic atmosphere, later known as Aestheticism, or more simply as "the Nineties."

This creed of self-redemption through art is related to the movements known as Symbolism and Impressionism. It is noteworthy that the Impressionist painters were able to take as subjects some of the sights that most depressed their fellow man and by recomposing them in brilliant, shimmering colour to create a refreshing world of new sensation. Subject once again mercifully disappeared. As Claude Monet said: "The principal subject in a painting is light."

The Symbolists in literature had a more difficult task than the painters, because their medium, words, must be shared with all those who speak the language for ordinary purposes. To disinfect grammar and vocabulary for poetry and "art prose" required severe measures. All set phrases had to be broken up, unusual words revived or common ones used in archaic or etymological senses; syntax had to be bent to permit fresh juxtapositions from which new meanings might emerge; above all, the familiar rhetoric and rhythms had to be avoided, until the literary work, poetry or prose, created the desired "new world." It is a world difficult to access but worth exploring, all its tangible parts being the symbols of a radiant reality beyond—in short, the antithesis of a newspaper editorial.

In music there was no need of any indirect device to establish the mood of Impressionism. It was already to be found here and there in the great Romantics, and when the new generation began to compose on themes drawn from contemporary literature, the hints and opportunities needed only a delicate genius to develop them into a style. Claude Debussy was that genius, soon followed by Maurice Ravel, Frederick Delius, Hugo Wolf, and others. Alike, yet independently of one another, they replaced eloquence, melodic clarity, and harmonic consecutiveness by capricious melodic contour and pointillist chord progressions to produce the shimmer and mystery of musical Impressionism.

AESTHETICISM

To those who dedicated their lives to Symbolist literature and criticism the name of aesthetes is often given, for it was at this time, from 1870 to the end of the century, that questions of aesthetics became the intense concern of artists, critics, and a portion of the public. The phrase "art for art's sake," which the Romanticists had toyed with, was revived and made the hallmark of high art. Whatever claimed the attention of the intellectual elite must receive this authentication, which guaranteed that no ulterior motive, such as propaganda, and no appeal to the middlebrow audience was discernible in the poem, painting, or musical composition. Common subject matter, ease of understanding, and accessibility were signs of compromise with vulgar taste. Having cut loose from evil society, art repudiated its former role of moral teacher and even of communicator; it was—or was to be—completely "autonomous," else it could not serve its devotees as a refuge from intolerable workaday existence.

Yet Aestheticism was by no means as languid and fatalistic as it tried to appear. Writers such as Oscar Wilde, George Moore, Stéphane Mallarmé, and Edmond and Jules Goncourt, though promoting the idea of art as spiritual shelter, took an active part in current affairs. Moore wrote naturalistic novels; Mallarmé gave interviews to the press and wrote advertisements for perfume and other luxuries; and Wilde, whom it is easy, because of his notoriety on many counts, to dismiss as colourful but ephemeral, was an effective propagandist in the assault on the Victorian ethos. He was not a symptom but the representative man. His book reviewing and critical essays, his story *The Picture of Dorian Gray*, his great *Ballad of Reading Gaol*, the autobiographical *De Profundis*, and the greatest farce in the language, *The Importance of Being Earnest*, together form a kind of sourcebook for the period and have also lasted as literature. What Wilde accomplished through these works was the liberation of English literature from ancestral (and not merely Victorian) preconceptions. He reconnected England with the Continent artistically by phrasing with finality their different assumptions. He showed that art could be morally responsible only by discarding moralism. In a word, he played again in 1890 the role Gautier had played in France in 1835 with his anti-bourgeois diatribe in *Mademoiselle de Maupin*. Whoever, starting with Wilde or Gautier, wishes to follow the historical sequence and recapture the atmosphere in which this activity went on will find no better source than the *Journal* of the Goncourts, who were the inventors of a mannered "art prose," of contemporary lives, characters, and gossip.

The reader of their voluminous pages will also find there references to the movement called Naturalism,

Irish writer and Aesthete Oscar Wilde. Alfred Ellis & Walery/Hulton Archive/Getty Images

which does not merely parallel but also intermingles with Symbolism and Impressionism. The Goncourts themselves wrote a number of Naturalistic novels; their friend Émile Zola was the theorist and greatest master of the genre; another novelist, Joris-Karl Huysmans, passed from Naturalism to Symbolism, as did several other writers. In the poets Arthur Rimbaud and Paul Verlaine, as later in the Irish poet William Butler Yeats, the elements of the two tendencies alternated or mixed.

NATURALISM

The name Naturalism suggests the philosophy of science, and the connection is genuine. Zola thought that in his great series of novels, *Les Rougon-Macquart*, he was studying the "natural and social history" of a family during the time of Napoleon III. The claim was bolstered by the method Zola used of gathering data like a scientist—every material fact could be proved by reference to actuality or statistics. Naturalism would thus appear to be an intensification of Realism, as indeed it was—more "research." It differed markedly in spirit, however. Realism professed to be the depiction of the commonplace through a mood of stoicism or indifference—a photographic plate from a camera held almost at random in front of unselected mediocrity; it was, as Flaubert was the first to say, a refusal to share previous Romanticist hopes and interests. Naturalism, on the contrary, readmitted purpose and selectivity. Each novel was a "study" designed to exhibit and denounce the dismal truths of social existence, for which purpose the worst are the best. Zola's novels throb with a passionate love of life, a life which he showed as tortured and twisted by character and condition. In the end he defined his scientific or "experimental" novel as "a corner of nature seen through a temperament." The aim of the Naturalists was not only to

Aristide Maillol's statue Venus with a Necklace, *c. 1918–28*. Roger Viollet/ Getty Images

show but to show up. They meant to teach the great prosperous middle class how those beneath them lived and even beyond that to disgust the sensitive with the human condition, whatever its social embodiment. In this effort it shares with the aesthetes the animus of denunciation.

In the plastic arts, a plausible counterpart of Naturalism is the work of those known as Postimpressionists, notably Paul Cézanne and Vincent van Gogh in painting, Auguste Rodin and Aristide Maillol in sculpture. Their various styles and aims had a common result in restoring solidity and "weight" to the visual object after the fluidity and lightness of Impressionism.

Musical naturalism was, by contrast, an attempt at dramatic literalness. Richard Strauss boasted that he could render a soup spoon. Actually, he could not and did not. The noises of his *Sinfonia Domestica* are standard orchestral sounds fitted with a preliminary explanation, like the libretto or synopsis of a Wagnerian or other opera. When the sheep bleat in Strauss's *Don Quixote*, the clarinets play notes that are decorative on their own account and do not in the least suggest wool. It is rather the thickness of Strauss's orchestration and chromatic harmony that connect him with naturalist doctrine—the headlong embrace with matter. And so it is also in the operas of Alfred Bruneau or Gustave Charpentier or in the *verismo* of Giacomo Puccini and the late Italian school generally. Music remains atmospheric; never, except in Wagner's system, denotative.

This definition of Naturalism, coupled with the aesthetic, or "art for art's sake," impetus in Symbolism and with the Impressionists' transmutation of concreteness into light, justifies the name of Neoromanticism that has been given to the cultural temper with which the 19th century ended. After the glum self-repression of the middle period, it was an outburst of vehement self-assertion, whether directed inward or outward. "Art for art's sake" and Naturalism are indeed but twin branches of one doctrine: art for life's sake.

THE NEW CENTURY

In 1895 George Bernard Shaw said: "France is certainly decadent if she thinks she is." The remark is characteristic of Shaw, but it is also indicative of a new wave of energy. From under the despair and decadence, the scattered retreats and the violent nihilism, the same human strength that produced Symbolist and Naturalist art was trying to reshape the civilization that all found so unsatisfactory.

In England, the Fabians, of whom Shaw was one, were preaching the "inevitableness of gradualism" toward the socialist state. It was they, seconded by the growing strength of the trade unions after a spectacular dock strike of 1889, who paved the way to Labour governments and the British welfare state. Throughout Europe, socialism was no longer the creed of a lunatic fringe but was the ideal of many among the masses and the intellectuals. The original fight for liberty and democracy in political action had turned into a fight for economic democracy—freedom from want. Laissez-faire liberalism had turned inside out, and the liberal imagination at work in the many brands of socialism now demanded state interference to remove the appalling conditions causing all the despair.

Arts and Crafts Movement

Among the socialists belonging to no party, Ruskin and William Morris worked also to effect immediate changes in the quality of their surroundings: they started the so-called Arts and Crafts movement, whose aim was to make objects once again beautiful. Because machine industry produced only the "cheap and nasty" (as it was commonly called), they tried to produce by hand the cheap and handsome—good furniture, hangings, and household articles; fast dyes of good colour; well-printed books on good paper; and jewelry and ornaments of all kinds that showed visual talent as well as manual skill. In a word, the movement reinstated the ideal of design and succeeded in forcing it on machine industry itself.

As approval of the Arts and Crafts movement widened, the movement became diffused and less specifically identified with a small group of people. Its ideas spread to other countries and became identified with the growing international interest in design, specifically with Art Nouveau. Manufacturers began hiring artists as designers, and by 1910 the 20th-century omnipresence of design, from clothes to print and from gadgetry to packaging, was a fait accompli. The visual revolution can be seen easily by looking back with modern eyes to a page of advertising at the turn of the century.

New Trends in Technology and Science

In parallel with the new craftsmanship, the new technology of the 1900s began to give hope of wider improvements. The use and transmission of electric power suggested the possibility of the clean factory, all glass and white tile. Better machines, new materials and alloys, a greatly expanded chemical industry—all supplied more exact, more functional, less hazardous objects of use and consumption, while the application of science to medicine nourished the hope of greatly reducing the physical ills of humankind. Those closest to all these developments were certainly not among the despairers

Art Nouveau

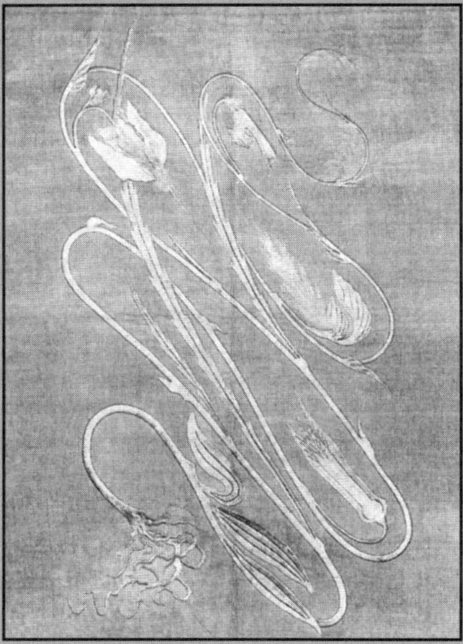

"The Whiplash," Art Nouveau tapestry by Hermann Obrist, silk embroidered on wool, 1895; in the Münchner Stadtmuseum, Munich. Courtesy of the Münchner Stadtmuseum, Munich

Art Nouveau is an ornamental style of art that flourished between about 1890 and 1910 throughout Europe and the United States. Art Nouveau is characterized by its use of a long, sinuous, organic line and was employed most often in architecture, interior design, jewelry and glass design, posters, and illustration. It was a deliberate attempt to create a new style, free of the imitative historicism that dominated much of 19th-century art and design. Art Nouveau developed first in England and soon spread to the European continent, where it was called Jugendstil in Germany, Sezessionstil in Austria, Stile Floreale (or Stile Liberty) in Italy, and Modernismo (or Modernista) in Spain. The term "Art Nouveau" was coined by a gallery in Paris that exhibited much of this work.

In England the style's immediate precursors were the Aestheticism of the illustrator Aubrey Beardsley, who depended heavily on the expressive quality of organic line, and the Arts and Crafts movement of William Morris, who established the importance of a vital style in the applied arts. On the European continent, Art Nouveau was also influenced by experiments with expressive line by the painters Paul Gauguin and Henri de Toulouse-Lautrec. The movement was also partly inspired by a vogue for the linear patterns of Japanese prints (ukiyo-e).

The distinguishing ornamental characteristic of Art Nouveau is its undulating, asymmetrical line, often taking the form of flower stalks and buds, vine tendrils, insect wings, and other delicate and sinuous natural objects; the line may be elegant and graceful or infused with a powerfully rhythmic and whiplike force. In the graphic arts the line subordinates all other pictorial elements—form, texture, space, and colour—to its own decorative effect. In architecture and the other plastic arts, the whole of the three-dimensional form becomes engulfed in the organic, linear rhythm, creating a fusion between structure and ornament. Architecture particularly shows this synthesis of ornament and structure; a liberal combination of materials—ironwork, glass, ceramic, and brickwork—was employed, for example, in the creation of unified interiors in which columns and beams became thick vines with spreading tendrils and windows became both openings for light and air and membranous outgrowths of the organic whole. This approach was directly opposed to the traditional architectural values of reason and clarity of structure.

There were a great number of artists and designers who worked in the Art Nouveau style. Some of the more prominent were the Scottish architect and designer Charles Rennie Mackintosh, who specialized in a predominantly geometric line and particularly influenced the Austrian Sezessionstil; the Belgian architects Henry van de Velde and Victor Horta, whose extremely sinuous and delicate structures influenced the French architect Hector Guimard, another important figure; the American glassmaker Louis Comfort Tiffany; the French furniture and ironwork designer Louis Majorelle; the Czechoslovakian graphic designer-artist Alphonse Mucha; the French glass and jewelry designer René Lalique; the American architect Louis Henry Sullivan, who used plantlike Art Nouveau ironwork to decorate his traditionally structured buildings; and the Spanish architect and sculptor Antonio Gaudí, perhaps the most original artist of the movement, who went beyond dependence on line to transform buildings into curving, bulbous, brightly coloured, organic constructions.

After 1910 Art Nouveau appeared old-fashioned and limited and was generally abandoned as a distinct decorative style. It was important, however, in moving toward the 20th-century aesthetic of unity of design.

and fugitives from the world. Like all those who struggle successfully with practical difficulties, they were inspirited by what they knew to be demonstrable progress along their chosen lines.

The same outlook animated workers in the natural and social sciences. It was for both a time of transformation, and genuine novelty exerted its usual invigorating effect. From the 1880s onward it had been clear that simple mechanistic explanations based on "dead" matter were inadequate. The Michelson-Morley experiment of 1887 had given the coup de grace to the mere push-pull principle by showing that, though light consisted of waves, the waves were not in or of anything, such as the ether, which did not exist. Even earlier, James Clerk Maxwell's attempt to work out the facts of electromagnetism on Newtonian principles had failed. And on the philosophic front, the notion of natural "laws" was being radically modified by thinkers such as Henri Poincaré, Émile Boutroux, Ernst Mach, Henri Bergson, and William James. All this prepared the ground for the twin revolutions of relativity and quantum theory on which the 20th-century scientific regime is based.

The decline of the machine analogy had its counterpart in the biological sciences. With narrow Darwinian dogmas in abeyance, the genetics of Gregor Mendel were rediscovered, and a new science was born. The fixity of species was again regarded as important (William Bateson), while the phenomenon of large mutations (Hugo de Vries) caught the public imagination, just as the slow, small changes had done 60 years earlier. The elusive "fitness of the environment" was being considered of as much importance in the march of evolution as the fitness of the creature. Vitalism once more reasserted its claims, as it seems bound to do in an eternal seesaw with mechanism.

The Social Sciences

Finally, in the social sciences, fresh starts were made on new premises. Anthropology dropped its concern with physique and race and turned to "culture" as the proper unit of scientific study. Similarly in sociology, Émile Durkheim, seconded by Ferdinand Tönnies, Max Weber, Gabriel Tarde, and Gustave Le Bon, concentrated on "the social fact" as an independent and measurable reality equivalent to a physical datum. Psychology, also long under the exclusive sway of physics and physiology, now established at the hands of William James that the irreducible element of its subject matter was the "stream of consciousness"—not a compound of atomized "ideas" or "impressions" or "mind-stuff" but a live force in which image and feeling, subconscious drive and purposive interest, were not separable except abstractly. A last domain of research was mythology, to the significance of which James George Frazer's *The Golden Bough* gave massive witness, thereby exerting proportional influence on literature and criticism.

Reexamination of the Universe

The net effect of these innovations in the sciences of society and of nature was liberating. Whatever each specialty or subspecialty meant to its practitioners, the persons who carry in their minds the general culture of an age took the new message to mean that the universe, formerly closed and complete like a machine, had been reopened and shown to be more alive than dead—and by the same token more mysterious, full of questions to be resolved by new research and new sciences. The term "astrophysics," replacing astronomy, symbolized the change of perspective from Isaac Newton's cosmology to Albert Einstein's. In turn, these conclusions furnished a new opportunity for the exercise of individual thought and will in the realm of mind and spirit, of ethics and religion. People were no longer deemed automatons—they had free choice in the all-important matters that lay outside physical science.

In philosophy, politics, and criticism this reexamination may be called the pragmatic revolution; in social and moral life, the liquidation of Victorianism. But the pragmatic revolution must not be thought of as being only the work of those who, like James, called themselves pragmatists. Nietzsche, Samuel Butler, Shaw, Bergson, and others constitute the headwaters of the stream of thought that issues in present-day existentialism. The common features are the turning away from absolutes and unities to pluralisms and the method of testing by consequences. Subjective and objective tests looking to future thought and action—not authority or antecedents—are to decide what is true, good, and beautiful.

Such an outlook, of which the refinements are, like the defects, beyond the scope of this book, is the logical and appropriate one for an age of reconstruction. It boils down to trying all things new and holding fast to that which is good, but it presupposes the creation of new things to try, and here it is allied to the liquidation of Victorianism. In morals the work of destruction generally begins by affirming the opposite of the accepted rule. An excellent source book for this attitude is Butler's *The Way of All Flesh*, written in 1885 but not published until 1903. The Victorian Tennyson had said: "'Tis better to have loved and lost than never to have loved at all." Butler said: "'Tis better to have loved and lost than never to have lost at all." This inversion of values—don't weep over loss; there are plenty of loves to be had and the more the merrier—is but an

British suffragist under arrest after participating in an attack on Buckingham Palace, London, in 1914. BBC Hutton Picture Library

indication of method. At first the denial was uttered as humour and paradox: Butler's *Note-books*, Shaw's *Arms and the Man* (the soldier wants chocolate, not ammunition), Wilde's *The Importance of Being Earnest*, Alfred Jarry's *Ubu roi*, August Strindberg's tragicomedies—to cite but a few subverters of the Victorian—all used derision and topsy-turviness to make their point.

Underneath the joke was the new purpose, which soon found open expression in positive utterance and action. In the plays of Gerhart Hauptmann and Eugène Brieux, the novels and anticipations of H.G. Wells, the essays of Leo Tolstoy, Charles Péguy, Georges Sorel, Ellen Key, Havelock Ellis, Miguel de Unamuno, José Ortega y Gasset, or Shaw, the new modes of feeling and the new scale of virtues and vices are set forth with as much earnestness and vigour as the old Victorian kind.

Nor did action wait until all the books were out. From the onset of the overturn, say 1885 onward, the rebellion was a biographical fact. Individuals braved public opinion and got divorced, lived together unmarried, practiced and preached contraception, studied the psychology of sex, and defended homosexuality. Or again, the sons of the rich turned socialist, became labour leaders, and fomented syndicalist (i.e., direct-action) strikes, while the daughters demanded the vote as suffragists, assaulted policemen, and went to jail for chaining themselves to the door handles of government offices. Meanwhile, students rioted about international incidents or university affairs; schools were subjected to the devastation of the softer pedagogies; "rational clothing" exhibited itself in spite of derision, like the bicycle and the newfangled automobile; and new cults multiplied like mushrooms—outdoor sports, nudism, Theosophy, Esoteric Buddhism, Rosicrucianism, New Thought, the Society for Psychical Research, Christian Science, the Salvation Army, and the "Maximinism" of Stefan George.

Of these, hardly any need explanation here. But a word must be added about Theosophy if only because of its historical importance in developing Yeats's genius and for expressing once again the attraction that the "wisdom of the East" has for Westerners. Not that the doctrine elaborated by Helena Blavatsky rested on any exact knowledge of Hindu religion and philosophy. That is not its point. The point is rather that Theosophy supplied the need for quietude, mystery, transcendence, and immortality in the wearied souls of Europeans. In Theosophy the doctrine of reincarnation offers satisfaction of immortal longings and inspires to wisdom, the demands of which are periodically revealed by mahatmas, or holy men.

As for the poet Stefan George's worship of his young friend Maximin, who died at age 15, it answers a similar

Theosophical Society

Founded in New York City in 1875 by Helena Blavatsky of Russia, the Theosophical Society was originally inspired by Kabbala (Jewish esoteric mysticism), Gnosticism (esoteric salvatory knowledge), and other forms of Western occultism. When Blavatsky went to India in 1879, her doctrines quickly took on an Indian character, and from her headquarters at Adyar she and her followers established branches in many cities of India.

After surviving serious accusations of charlatanry leveled against its founder and other leaders, the society prospered under the leadership of Annie Besant, a reform-minded Englishwoman. During her tenure the many Theosophical lodges founded in Europe and the United States helped to acquaint the West with the principles of Hinduism, if in a rather idiosyncratic form.

impulse to permanent truth but with the additional urge to abolish (rather than escape) "contemporary materialism." George was but one among many European writers who wanted to found a new society in place of the actual one. What has fitly been called the politics of cultural despair found new hope in a number of possible saviours—monarchy, "integral nationalism," a new aristocracy (usually tinged with intellect), technocracy (rule by science and the engineers), the proletariat (in syndicalist "cells" or communist collectives), trade and professional guilds federated in a corporate state, or again the mystic unity of "blood" and "race." In all these creeds, at least at their beginnings, the thirst for the ideal is evident. Together they formed a new utopianism, of which the later fruits are familiar but quite other than those predicted: Soviet and Chinese communism, Italian fascism, German National Socialism. The echoes and offshoots of this earlier wave of cultist thought are still found in many places. Attitudes and practices derived from the East (Zen, yoga, meditation) are taken for granted as permanent elements of Western pluralist culture, part of the broad offering of "lifestyles."

In one country, as the 19th century passed into the 20th, all the violent rival energies seeking an ideal found an unexpected outlet. The occasion for battle was the conviction of a French officer for espionage; i.e., the Dreyfus affair. Its cultural suggestiveness is apparent: on one side, the ideal of justice and the regard for the individual as an end in himself; on the other, the social or collective ideal typified by the army and the nation. Facts were pursued, lost, and found again in an embittered struggle that threw up a host of endemic prejudices about race, about class, and about intellect—to say nothing of individual egotisms and obsessions that had been charged with the force of pent-up aggression. Yet throughout the affair, for both sides, the ultimate quest was the ideal of truth.

THE PREWAR PERIOD

The same universal aggressiveness was to have its field day in the coming war of nations, but in the intervening decade (1905–14) occurred the remarkable outburst of a creativeness, which, for the first time since 1789, had its source elsewhere than in Romanticism. The "Cubist decade" (as it has been conveniently called) gave the models and the methods of a new art, just as the natural and social sciences had begun to do for themselves a little earlier. Cubism in painting defined itself as a new Classicism, but it was obviously not Neoclassical. In painting and sculpture, in music and poetry, and in architecture especially, the new qualities were simplicity, abstraction, and the importance of mass.

This truly modern art evidently meant to reconnect itself to contemporary life. To define it in one word, it was Constructivist. As such, it valued the products of technology, which embodied artists' rediscovered love of matter and from which they drew suggestions of form. In the style of interior furnishing known as Art Deco, geometric angularity, smooth surfaces, plain glass, and strong colours not only matched the unadorned outside of buildings in the new International Style but also resembled the creations of the industrial engineers. Indeed, it was not unusual to see on the mantelpiece of an Art Deco living room a set of gears or some other portion of a modern machine. The latest sculptures on western streets are but a further fragmentation of the new taste for solidity, clarity, volume, and mass.

To this many-sided, original, and buoyant productiveness the war of 1914 put an instantaneous stop. It was a war of a sort Europe had not known since 1815—the nation in arms. And at that earlier time, the absence of large industry had precluded the involvement, physical and mental, of every adult citizen simultaneously throughout Europe. In 1914 Ludwig van Beethoven and Johann Wolfgang von Goethe, William Wordsworth and Eugène Delacroix would have been in the trenches.

The cessation of cultural activities; their replacement everywhere by a propaganda of hate; the rapid decimation of talent and genius in the murderous warfare of bombardment and infantry assault; the gradual demoralization through four years of less and less intelligible war aims; and after the Armistice, the long sequel of horrors—starvation, dispersion, disease, and massacre—together shattered the high civilization born of the Renaissance and based on the idea of the national state. Too many able men and women had been killed for the continuity of culture. Too many intimate faiths and civil traditions had been ground down for any recovery of self-confidence and public hope to be possible.

CHAPTER 6

Society and Culture Amid the World Wars, 1914–45

Rapid change was the hallmark of many aspects of life from 1914 to 1945, and nowhere was it more apparent than in Europe. Photographs from 1914 preserve a period appearance ever more archaic: statesmen in frock coats and top hats; early automobiles that fit their contemporary description as "horseless carriages"; biplane "flying machines" with open cockpits; long, voluminous bathing costumes. The young 20th century, its advent celebrated in such enterprises as The New Century Library—pocket editions of classics recently out of copyright—appears in such images more and more like a mere continuation of the century before.

The 19th century had itself seen the culmination of the Industrial Revolution that had begun in the 18th, but the transformation wrought by steam power, steel, machine-made textiles, and rail communications was only the beginning. Still more rapid and spectacular changes came with further advances in science and technology: electricity, telegraphy and telephony, radio and television, subatomic physics, oil and petrochemicals, plastics, jet engines, computers, telematics, and bioengineering.

The development of technology, in particular, would not have been possible without a more skilled and better educated work force. In most European countries during this period, education was extended both to more of the population and to a later age, and the numbers entering higher education greatly increased. Women began to gain access to more of the opportunities hitherto monopolized by men.

If this was a process of social leveling upward, the same process began to affect the social classes themselves. While European society remained more hierarchical than that in the United States, there began to be both greater social mobility and fewer blatant class differences as expressed in clothes, behaviour, and speech. A "mass society" began to share mass pleasures. Apparent homogeneity, both vertically within societies and horizontally between them, was accelerated by the cinema, radio, and television, each offering attractive role models to be imitated or, by older generations, deplored. Some referred to this process as "the Americanization of Europe."

Alongside these changes, and in some instances spurring them, the period of 1914–45 in Europe has been marked by major economic and political upheavals. The most cataclysmic were the two world wars. The second of these resulted from the rise of dictatorship in Italy and Germany, but the period also saw dictatorships in Spain and Portugal, as well as in the U.S.S.R., where the 1917 revolution was followed by the totalitarian rule of Joseph Stalin.

The two wars, of 1914–18 and 1939–45, brought the old Europe of the balance of power to the brink of destruction. Europeans were thenceforth spectators at or minor actors in the global balance of terror between the United States and the U.S.S.R. This convinced a number of European statesmen that their peace, prosperity, and position in the world could be safeguarded only if Europeans united.

THE GREAT WAR, OR WORLD WAR I

Engulfing nearly all of Europe, the First World War was waged between the Central Powers—Germany, Austria-Hungary, and Turkey—and the Allied Powers—mainly France, Britain, Russia, Italy, Japan, and (from 1917) the

United States. After a Serbian nationalist assassinated Archduke Francis Ferdinand of Austria in June 1914, a chain of threats and mobilizations resulted in a general war between the antagonists by mid-August. Prepared to fight a war on two fronts, based on the Schlieffen Plan, Germany first swept through neutral Belgium and invaded France. After the First Battle of the Marne (1914), the Allied defensive lines were stabilized in France, and a war of attrition began. Fought from lines of trenches and supported by modern artillery and machine guns, infantry assaults gained little ground and were enormously costly in human life, especially at the Battles of Verdun and the Somme (1916). On the Eastern Front, Russian forces initially drove deep into East Prussia and German Poland (1914) but were stopped by German and Austrian forces at the Battle of Tannenberg and forced back into

Austrian Archduke Francis Ferdinand rides through Sarajevo with his wife, Sophie, on June 28, 1914, shortly before both were assassinated. Henry Guttmann/Hulton Archive/Getty Images

Russia (1915). After several offensives, the Russian army failed to break through the German defensive lines. Russia's poor performance and enormous losses caused widespread domestic discontent that led to the Russian Revolution of 1917. Other fronts in the war included the Dardanelles Campaign, in which British and Dominion forces were unsuccessful against Turkey; the Caucasus and Iran (Persia), where Russia fought Turkey; Mesopotamia and Egypt, where British forces fought the Turks; and northern Italy, where Italian and Austrian troops fought the costly Battles of the Isonzo. At sea, the German and British fleets fought the inconclusive Battle of Jutland, and Germany's use of the submarine against neutral shipping eventually brought the United States into the war in 1917. Though Russia's armistice with Germany in December 1917 released German troops to fight on the Western Front, the Allies were reinforced by U.S. troops in early 1918. Germany's unsuccessful offensive in the Second Battle of the Marne was countered by the Allies' steady advance, which recovered most of France and Belgium by October 1918 and led to the November Armistice.

THE CULTURAL SHOCK OF THE FIRST WORLD WAR

The year 1914 witnessed not only the outbreak of World War I but also such very different events as the publication of James Joyce's short stories *Dubliners*, André Gide's novel *Les Caves du Vatican*, and D.H. Lawrence's story "The Prussian Officer". It was also the year of Pablo Picasso's painting *The Small Table*, Igor Stravinsky's *Rossignol*, Serge Diaghilev's ballet version of Nikolay Rimsky-Korsakov's *Le Coq d'or*, and the founding of the Vorticist movement in Britain by the painter and writer Percy Wyndham Lewis.

All these, in their various ways, were characteristically "modern" phenomena. The new century had already produced some fairly self-conscious attempts to criticize or repudiate the past. In 1901 the novelist Thomas Mann had chronicled in *Buddenbrooks* the decline of a Lübeck business family as it became more "refined," while in Sweden the playwright August Strindberg had savagely dissected in *The Dance of Death* a love-hate relationship on the eve of a silver wedding anniversary.

In 1903 Samuel Butler's bitter semi-autobiographical *The Way of All Flesh* had been posthumously published.

Scene from a performance of August Strindberg's The Dance of Death. Lipnitzki/Roger Viollet/Getty Images

In 1904 Frank Wedekind had fiercely attacked social and sexual hypocrisy in his play *Pandora's Box*. In 1905, Thomas Mann's brother Heinrich had shown a tyrannical schoolmaster ruined by an affair with a nightclub singer in *Professor Unrat* (better known in its 1928 film version as *The Blue Angel*). In 1907 the respectable writer and critic Edmund Gosse had anonymously published *Father and Son*, an autobiography recording what he called "a struggle between two temperaments, two consciences and almost two epochs."

In that same year (1907), Picasso and Georges Braque had founded the Cubist movement, with its slogan, "Paint not what you see but what you know is there." In 1909 *La Nouvelle Revue française* had been inaugurated as a forum for younger writers. In 1910 Wassily Kandinsky had produced a Postimpressionist painting defiantly entitled *First Abstract Work*; the Russian authorities had banned Rimsky-Korsakov's two-year-old *Le Coq d'or* because of its satire on government; and Sir Norman Angell had published *The Great Illusion*—an attempt to demonstrate the futility of war, even for the supposed victors. The year 1913, finally, had seen the publication of Guillaume Apollinaire's poems *Alcoöls* and the beginning of Marcel Proust's great novel *Remembrance of Things Past*.

The 20th century had begun, then, with what might be termed cultural parricide—an attack on the paternalistic, stuffily religious, and sexually repressive features of the century before. Younger writers and artists such as Joyce, Lawrence, Gide, Picasso, Stravinsky, Diaghilev, Wyndham Lewis, Ezra Pound, and T.S. Eliot formed what the novelist Ford Madox Ford called "a proud and haughty generation," determined, in Pound's words, to "make it new." Yet, looking back in 1937, Wyndham Lewis wrote ruefully:

We are not only "the last men of an epoch" (as Mr Edmund Wilson and others have said): we are more than that, or we are that in a different way to what is most often asserted. We are the first men of a Future that has not materialised.

What had blocked that future was war—"The Great War," as its stunned contemporaries called it. Not for nothing did the poet and novelist Robert Graves call his 1929 war reminiscences *Good-bye to All That*. He was bidding farewell to his prewar schooldays and to his first marriage; but what stuck in the minds of his readers was the cause of the leave-taking—the horror of life and death in the trenches of the Western Front. Graves was by no means the only writer to experience and report that visceral shock. In 1914, despite Angell's warnings, the idea of war had still borne vestiges of glamour. Idealistic young poets such as Rupert Brooke and Julian Grenfell had gone to war, initially, with eager innocence. After the slaughter on the Somme and the stalemate of trench warfare, the key word became *Disenchantment*, the apt title of C.E. Montague's account of the process. It pervaded the work of Edmund Blunden, Siegfried Sassoon, and Wilfred Owen in Britain, of Henri Barbusse (author of *Under Fire*) in France, and of Erich Maria Remarque (author of *All Quiet on the Western Front*) in Germany.

Through conscription, and, to a lesser extent, through air raids, the war had involved and affected far more of the population than any previous international conflict. By the time of the Armistice, in November 1918, there was widespread weariness in Europe and a sense of disillusion that gave the years before the war a retrospective autumn radiance, as if a dream had died.

Real deaths, indeed, had been numbered in millions. In the whole of the previous century, from the Napoleonic

Wars to the Balkan Wars of 1912–1913, Europe had lost fewer than 4.5 million men. Now, at least 8 million had died in four years, while more than twice as many had been wounded, some of them crippled for life. Millions more had succumbed to the worldwide influenza epidemic that had ended in 1918. The outcome, in all countries, was imbalance between the sexes—a shortage of men that at the time was sometimes called "the problem of surplus women." During the war, women had had to be recruited into the civilian work force—in factories "for the duration," in offices sometimes for good. The net result was to encourage women's emancipation. In 1918, British women over the age of 30 were given the vote—although women's suffrage was delayed until 1944 in France and 1945 in Italy. The year 1921, moreover, saw the opening of the first birth control clinic in Britain.

Wartime comradeship helped to reduce not only barriers between the sexes but also rigidities of class. Government control of the war economy—known in Germany as *Kriegssozialismus*, or war socialism—was also a general phenomenon that left a permanent mark, especially encouraging economic nationalism. Nowhere was this process more intense than in Russia after the Bolshevik Revolution of November 1917, where it was known as "war communism."

Nationalism had been a feature of Europe since at least the French Revolution. Napoleon had embodied its classic, democratic, or Gallic variety—the nation as a people bearing arms. Equally powerful, and more deeply rooted in history, was Romantic, cultural, or Germanic nationalism—the nation as an entity based on age-old racial and linguistic allegiance. Both forms of nationalism were encouraged by the war and its aftermath, and the latter was especially furthered by some of the provisions in the Treaty of Versailles.

THE INTERWAR YEARS

The peace conference that met in Paris from January 1919 to January 1920 and which produced, among other things, the Treaty of Versailles, was both vengeful and idealistic. Public opinion in France and Britain wished to impose harsh terms, especially on Germany. French military circles sought not only to recover Alsace and Lorraine and to occupy the Saar but also to detach the Rhineland from Germany. Members of the British Parliament lobbied to increase the reparations Germany was to pay, despite the objections of several farsighted economists, including John Maynard Keynes.

The Versailles treaty, signed on June 28, 1919, met most of these demands. It also stripped Germany of its colonies and imposed severe restrictions on the rebuilding of its army and fleet. In these ways, the peace settlement could be seen as punishing the defeated enemy, as well as reducing its status and strength. Not unnaturally, this caused resentment among the Germans and helped to stimulate the quest for revenge.

At the same time, however, Versailles was imbued with more constructive aims and hopes. In January 1918 the U.S. president, Woodrow Wilson, set out his peace proposals in the "Fourteen Points." The general principles were open covenants openly arrived at, freedom of navigation, equality of trading conditions, the reduction of armaments, and the adjustment of colonial claims. Wilson also proposed "a general association," which became the League of Nations, but his more specific suggestions were concerned less with unity among nations than with national self-determination. His aim, in effect, was to secure justice, peace, and democracy by making the countries of Europe more perfect nation-states.

Among other measures, this involved readjusting Germany's borders. Alsace-Lorraine was duly returned to France and Eupen-Malmédy to Belgium, while Germany also lost territory to the east. But the Versailles and associated settlements went further still in dealing with central Europe. They broke up the Austro-Hungarian Empire, they created or re-created sovereign states, and they sought to make frontiers coincide with the boundaries between ethnic, linguistic, and cultural groups. This consecration of nationalism proved a highly equivocal legacy—for example, in Northern Ireland or in the German-speaking Sudetenland of Bohemia.

In succession to the Habsburg empire, Austria and Hungary became small, separate, landlocked states. Poland was restored and acquired new territory; so did Greece, Italy, and Romania, which doubled its former size. Czechoslovakia and Yugoslavia came into existence as composite states. Estonia, Latvia, and Lithuania won independence from Russia.

Parallel to the dismemberment of the Austro-Hungarian Empire, a further result of the war was the collapse of the Ottoman Empire. Most of its eastern Mediterranean territory, together with Iraq, was placed under mandate to France and to Britain, which backed a ring of Arab sheikdoms around the Persian Gulf, the Red Sea, and the Indian Ocean. Turkey was reduced to a mere 300,000 square miles. The peace terms initially agreed upon by the Treaty of Sèvres were rejected by the sultan until British troops occupied Istanbul, and even then the National Assembly in Ankara organized resistance. A war with Greece in 1921–22 ended in the Peace of Lausanne, giving Turkey better terms than those decided at Sèvres. Soon, however, the secular sultanate and the religious caliphate were abolished, and Kemal Atatürk became president of a new, secular republic, which, among other Westernizing measures, adopted the Latin alphabet in place of Arabic script.

The drawing of new frontiers could never definitively satisfy those who lived on either side of them, and the problem of minorities became an important factor in the instability that marked Europe after World War I. The new composite state of Czechoslovakia, for instance, included not only industrialized Bohemia, formerly Austrian, but also rustic Slovakia and Ruthenia, formerly Hungarian. Romania similarly comprised both Transylvania, formerly Hungarian, and Bessarabia, formerly Russian. Reconstituted Poland was equally an amalgam, and in 1921, after Józef Piłsudski's campaign against the U.S.S.R., it moved its eastern frontier more than 100 miles beyond the so-called Curzon Line established in 1920. Yugoslavia, finally, was based mainly on Serbia, but it also included Westernized Croatia, formerly Austro-Hungarian, and part of Easternized Macedonia, formerly Turkish, as well as other territories. The rest of Macedonia was now Greek, but an exchange of minorities between Greece and Bulgaria put many Macedonians under Bulgarian rule, sparking off an armed rebellion. Similar turbulence agitated Albania. Altogether, the Balkans became a synonym for violent nationalistic unrest.

Two global developments, moreover, formed an ominous backdrop to Europe's territorial disputes. One was the Russian Revolution of 1917, which inspired a few idealists but mainly aroused fear throughout the rest of Europe lest bolshevism spread westward. The other was the active intervention of the United States, which had entered the war—decisively—in 1917 and played a determinant role in shaping the peace.

Hopes in Geneva

Woodrow Wilson's vision of a general association of nations took shape in the League of Nations, founded in 1920. Its basic constitution was the Covenant—Wilson's word, chosen, as he said, "because I am an old Presbyterian." The Covenant was embodied in the Versailles and other peace treaties. The League's institutions, established in Geneva, consisted of an Assembly, in which each member country had a veto and an equal vote, and a smaller Council of four permanent members and four (later six, then nine) temporary members chosen by the Assembly.

The basic principle of the League was collective security, whereby its signatories were pledged both to seek peaceful solutions to disputes and to assist each other against

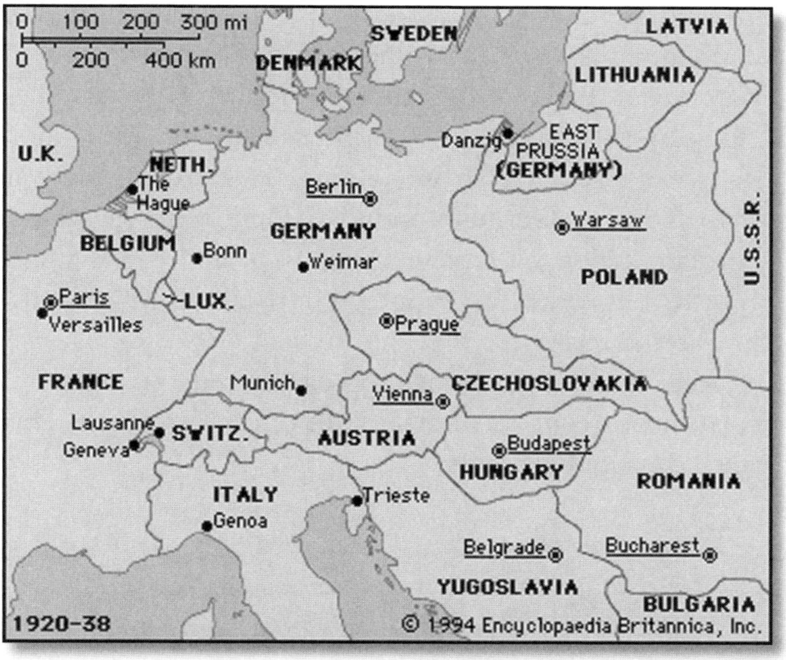

Europe, 1920–38.

aggression. As such, it was novel and potentially far-reaching; it could have developed into a powerful instrument for peace. It did indeed settle a number of practical disputes—between Finland and Sweden, Albania and Yugoslavia, Poland and Germany, Hungary and Czechoslovakia. It also set up subordinate bodies to deal with particular problems, among them the status of Danzig and the Saar, narcotics, refugees, and leprosy. It was complemented by a Permanent Court of International Justice in The Hague and by the International Labor Organization.

Yet the League of Nations disappointed its founders' hopes. From the start it lacked teeth, and most of its members were unwilling to see it develop. It thus became little more than a permanent version of the congresses (of Vienna, etc.) that had founded the old-style Concert of Europe.

Its first weakness was the veto: all its decisions had to be unanimous, or at least unopposed. Secondly, when in March 1920 the U.S. Congress failed to ratify the Versailles treaty by the necessary two-thirds majority, the United States was debarred from joining the League. Nor, at that time, were Germany and Russia among its members. Germany belonged from 1926 to 1933, and the U.S.S.R. from 1934 to 1939. Turkey joined in 1932, but Brazil withdrew in 1926, Japan in 1933, and Italy in 1937.

American suspicion of the League, reflecting general isolationism, centred on Article 10 of the Covenant. This called on member states

> *to respect and preserve as against external aggression the territorial integrity and existing political independence of all the Members of the League. In case of any such aggression or in case of any threat or danger of such aggression the Council shall advise upon the means by which this obligation shall be fulfilled.*

The means envisaged were known as sanctions—an economic boycott authorized under Article 16 of the Covenant and invoked in October 1935 against Italy for invading Abyssinia. However, as a conciliatory gesture, the League excluded oil, iron, and steel from the boycott, making the sanctions ineffective. Within less than a year they were lifted, and they were not applied at all when Germany sent troops into the Rhineland in 1936.

Nevertheless, the League did witness one effort to go beyond mere cooperation between governments. It proved abortive, but in retrospect it was highly significant. This was the proposal for European unity made by the French statesman Aristide Briand.

When taking office as foreign minister in 1925 he had declared his ambition to establish "a United States of Europe," and on Sept. 9, 1929, he made a speech to the then 27 European members of the League in which he proposed a federal union. Seven months later, on May 1, 1930, he laid before them a closely and cogently argued "Memorandum from the French Government on the Organization of a Regime of European Federal Union." The text was elegantly worded; its actual author was the secretary-general of the French Foreign Ministry, Alexis Léger—better known to readers of poetry under his pen name Saint-John Perse and later a winner of the Nobel Prize for Literature.

Briand's proposal evoked "the very real feeling of collective responsibility in the face of the danger that threatens the peace of Europe," and the need to counter Europe's "territorial fragmentation" by a "bond of solidarity which would enable European nations at last to take account of Europe's geographical unity." To this end, Briand proposed a pact establishing a European Conference within the League of Nations, with a permanent political committee and a small secretariat, putting politics before economics in this European community, but nevertheless working toward a "common market" in which "the movement of goods, capital, and people" would be gradually liberalized and simplified. The practical details, Briand suggested, should be worked out by the governments concerned.

Briand's Memorandum was careful to specify that agreement between the European nations must be reached on the basis of "absolute sovereignty and total political independence":

> *Is it not the genius of each nation to be able to affirm itself still more consciously by co-operating in the collective effort within a federal union that fully respects the traditions and characteristics of each of its constituent peoples?*

Despite these precautions, the other members of the League did little to implement the French initiative. Except for Bulgaria, Yugoslavia, and (with some reservations) Czechoslovakia, Greece, and Norway, their general response was at best skeptical and at worst politely hostile. None save the Netherlands saw any need to limit or pool national sovereignty. Many—including Denmark, Italy, the Netherlands, Poland, Sweden, Switzerland, and the United Kingdom—expressed fears for the integrity of the League. Several saw no point in setting up new institutions. Some wanted to recruit other European nations such as the U.S.S.R. and Turkey, which were not then members of the League; others insisted on their own world responsibilities, as did the United Kingdom. A large number—understandably, after the Wall Street crash—thought that Europe's really urgent tasks were economic, not political.

Briand defended his paper with vigour, but on Sept. 8, 1930, the European members of the League effectively buried it, with a few rhetorical flowers—"close collaboration," "in full agreement with the League of Nations," "respecting all the principles of the Pact"—by voting to put it on the agenda of the plenary Assembly. All that followed was a series of meetings, which ended with Briand's death in 1932.

Earlier, Briand had worked closely with the German foreign minister Gustav Stresemann, with whom he had negotiated the Locarno Treaties of 1925, confirming, among other things, the new western frontiers of Germany. A fervent nationalist during the war, Stresemann had come to the conclusion that Germany must respect the Versailles treaty, however harsh its provisions, though initially he had hoped to revise it. As a champion of peace (for which he had won the Nobel Prize in 1926), he would surely have supported Briand's federal union plan. But Stresemann died in 1929, and Chancellor Heinrich Brüning of the Catholic Centre Party proved no less negative than most of his colleagues elsewhere. By that time, too, Germany's fragile postwar Weimar Republic was under growing threat of collapse.

The Lottery in Weimar

Germany's Weimar Republic was born of defeat, revolution, and civil war. It was plagued by political violence but distinguished by cosmopolitan culture that influenced both Europe and the wider world.

On Oct. 28, 1918, the sailors at the Kiel naval base mutinied, and on November 8 the Independent Socialist Kurt Eisner declared Bavaria a republic. On the following day the chancellor, Prince Maximilian von Baden, resigned in favour of the Social Democrat leader Friedrich Ebert and announced the abdication of the emperor William II. That same day, November 9, the Social Democrat Philipp Scheidemann proclaimed all of Germany a republic. Two days later, on November 11, Germany concluded the Armistice that ended World War I.

The new republic was soon under pressure from both left and right. Left-wing socialists and Marxist "Spartacists," led by Karl Liebknecht and Rosa Luxemburg, fomented strikes and founded Workers' and Soldiers' Councils like those in the U.S.S.R., but on Jan. 15, 1919, both revolutionaries were arrested and brutally killed. On the right, meanwhile, ex-officers and others formed the paramilitary Freikorps. In the event, it was from the right that the deadliest challenges came.

Elections to a constitutional convention, or assembly, were held on Jan. 19, 1919. They gave the Social Democrats 163 seats, the Catholic Centre Party 89, and the new and progressive Democratic Party 75; other parties won smaller numbers of seats. These three groups were like-minded enough to form a coalition and powerful enough—for the present—to dominate the new republic. Their rivals on the right were the old conservatives (now called the National People's Party), with 42 seats, and the new People's Party, with 21. On the left, the Independent Socialists had 22 seats.

The National Assembly met on Feb. 6, 1919, at Weimar on the Ilm River. The choice of venue was only partly a tribute to the city's historic associations with Johann Wolfgang von Goethe, Friedrich von Schiller, and Johann Gottfried von Herder; the main concern was to avoid the danger of violence in Berlin. Not until the spring of 1920 did the new republic's Parliament (still called the Reichstag, or "Imperial Diet") meet in the German capital. By then, the name Weimar Republic had stuck.

Its constitution, completed on July 31, 1919, was the most modern and democratic imaginable, based on universal suffrage, proportional representation, and referenda. But it was a flimsy cap over a political volcano.

The first sign of trouble, in March 1920, was an attempted monarchist coup d'état. It failed, but the elections that followed in June marked a defeat for the republicans. The centrist Democrats lost almost two-thirds of their strength and the Social Democrats almost half of theirs. The right-wing parties and the left-wing Independent Socialists, plus various splinter groups, made heavy gains. The Weimar coalition no longer had a majority. Within the Parliament, the extremists had triumphed. Outside it, violence was on the increase.

On Aug. 26, 1921, two ex-officers shot and killed Matthias Erzberger, a Catholic Centre Party deputy who had negotiated the peace terms. On June 24, 1922, three right-wing students shot dead Walther Rathenau, the newly appointed foreign minister, who was Jewish. On Nov. 8–9, 1923, an extremist group staged an abortive *putsch* in Munich. The conspirators included Hermann Göring and Adolf Hitler.

Racked by economic problems, shaken by internal crises and shifting alliances, reviled by the far left and the far right, successive centrist governments struggled ahead for another 10 years. Although politically precarious, the Weimar Republic nonetheless witnessed and helped to foster an extraordinary explosion of creative talent, notably in the arts. Wassily Kandinsky and Max Ernst in painting, Bruno Walter in music, Bertolt Brecht and Max Reinhardt in the theatre, Walter Gropius in architecture, Albert Einstein in physics, Erwin Panofsky in art history, Ernst Cassirer in philosophy, Paul Tillich in theology, Wolfgang Köhler in psychology, Fritz Lang in film—all these became household names, partly because every one of them took refuge abroad after Hitler came to power in 1933.

All, in their various ways, were part of the cosmopolitan "Modern movement" that pervaded the whole of Europe.

Kandinsky was a typical example. Born in Russia, he learned a great deal from French Fauves such as André Derain and Henri Matisse, then settled in Munich, where he developed his own characteristic style. German Expressionist theatre and cinema, likewise, drew inspiration from abroad, in particular from Henrik Ibsen and August Strindberg. Germany was equally influenced by Austrians: Sigmund Freud in psychiatry, Hugo von Hofmannsthal and Arthur Schnitzler in the theatre, and Karl Kraus in the press. In architecture, the clean, functional lines of Gropius's Bauhaus school found imitators throughout Europe.

Like all such phenomena, the Modern movement was not wholly novel. Many of its practitioners and their artifacts had predated or coincided with World War I. Even Filippo Tommaso Marinetti's Futurism, so dominant in 1920s Italy, was a relic of the prewar past.

But the mood after 1918 was no longer so euphoric as at the beginning of the century. Before the war, the French novelist André Gide and the German poet Rainer Maria Rilke had exchanged letters in leisurely French like two survivors from the 18th century. After it, following a six-year silence, Rilke wrote of "the crumbling of a world," and both complained of the complications caused by passports and frontier formalities, looking back nostalgically to the carefree "journeys of long ago."

The postwar world, as seen by writers and other artists, had the fragmentary, disillusioned quality of T. S. Eliot's *The Waste Land,* published in 1922. It was self-conscious and introspective, as in Luigi Pirandello's 1921 play *Six Characters in Search of an Author*. It was more open to the unconscious, as in Dada and Surrealism. It was more aware of humans' dark fears and instincts, as in Franz Kafka's *The Trial* (1925) and *The Castle* (1926). It was more responsive to the appeal of "the primitive," whether in

African sculpture or in jazz—the quintessential art of the 1920s, which also influenced mainstream music, notably in the Austrian composer Ernst Krenek's 1927 opera *Jonny spielt auf* ("Johnny Strikes up the Band").

No less pervasive, however, was the brittle hedonism typified by the gossip-column antics of the "Bright Young Things." They were not wholly isolated. Already in 1918 Thomas Mann had published his *Reflections by an Unpolitical Man*; this was a mental label thankfully worn by many who, after the rigours of war, were eager to pursue private happiness, whether in metropolitan society or in placid suburbia. The Europe of Weimar also was the Europe of the detective story and the crossword puzzle. Both were analgesics at a time of political uncertainty and economic disquiet.

The Impact of the Slump

Economically, Europe emerged from World War I much weakened, partly by the purchases that had had to be made in the United States. Even in 1914 the United States had been the world's leading economic power. By 1918 profits had enabled it to invest more than $9 billion abroad, compared with $2.5 billion before the war. The Allies, meanwhile, had used up much of the capital they had invested in the United States and had accumulated large public debts, many of them to the U.S. Treasury.

American financial dominance and European debt overshadowed economic relations in the first decade after the war. The debts included those owed by the Allies to each other, especially to Britain, as well as those owed, especially by Britain, to the United States. A third baneful factor was reparations, the financial penalties imposed on Germany by the Treaty of Versailles.

Keynes described reparations as morally detestable, politically foolish, and economically nonsensical. Winston Churchill called them "a sad story of complicated idiocy." Essentially, they meant demanding from Germany either goods—which would have dislocated industry in the recipient countries—or money. This the Germans could obtain only by contracting vast and almost unrepayable loans in the United States—to whom the European recipients of reparations promptly returned much of the cash in an effort to settle their own transatlantic debts.

In April 1921 the Allied Reparations Committee set Germany's reparations bill at 132 billion gold marks, to be increased later if the Germans proved able to pay more. The first installment of one billion gold marks was due by the end of May.

Understandably resentful, the Germans wavered between two possible responses: refusal to pay, as urged by ultra-nationalists and some industrialists, and the so-called *Erfüllungspolitik*, or "policy of fulfillment," advocated by Rathenau and Stresemann. They proposed to meet initial demands for reparations so as to reestablish trust and then negotiate for better terms. This was the policy adopted by the Weimar Republic.

Even so, Germany paid the first tranche only in August 1921, in response to a threat to occupy the Ruhr, and the money had to come from a bank loan raised in London. Thereafter, it paid in kind but not in cash, until at the beginning of 1923 it announced that payments must cease. The French and the Belgians, backed by Italy but opposed by the United States and Britain, thereupon occupied the whole of the Ruhr.

With the German government's connivance, Ruhr industrialists and workers brought production to a virtual halt, and the Treasury printed a reckless flood of paper money. By 1924 the mark was almost worthless, enriching speculators and owners of real property but ruining rentier savers and others on fixed incomes. This removed an important stabilizer from German society, making it all the easier for extremism to triumph in the Nazi victory 10 years later.

For the moment, however, the Allies formed a committee of financial experts, chaired by the American Charles G. Dawes, to find a lasting solution to the reparations problem. It proposed, and the governments accepted, a two-year moratorium, the return of the Ruhr to Germany, a foreign loan of 800 million marks, and a new rate for reparation payments: 1–2.5 billion gold marks annually, which continued for five years. In 1929 a further committee, chaired by Owen D. Young, revised the Dawes Plan. Germany was to have a new loan of 1.2 billion marks and to spread reparations over the next 59 years. Although the German Parliament and people (by referendum) reluctantly agreed to the Young Plan, reparations finally ceased in 1932.

Germany's was an extreme case, but it was not the only European country to suffer after World War I. The Allies also experienced inflation and were saddled with debts. While the United States was willing in the long run to write off the political debts of reparations, it would not do the same with the commercial debts contracted by Britain, Italy, and France: one by one, they had to sign agreements to pay.

Despite these obligations, Europe in the 1920s enjoyed a modicum of the economic growth that was so rapid and spectacular in the United States. In 1913, Britain's income had been £2.021 billion. By 1921, it had fallen to £1.804 billion; but by 1929 it had risen again, this time to £2.319 billion. The corresponding figures for France (in 1938 francs) were 328 billion, 250 billion, and 453 billion. Even Germany, whose 1914 income had been

45.7 billion gold marks, had recovered enough by 1931 to be earning 57.5 billion.

Yet postwar prosperity was precarious. The American boom was a speculative affair. Fueled by optimism, production was soaring. To shift the accumulating goods, customers were urged to buy on credit or to borrow from the banks, which thereby earned large profits. The stock market was riding high. But at any sign of a credit squeeze or a loss of confidence, everything was likely to collapse. Demand would fall, goods would pile up, and prices would plummet. This was precisely what happened on "Black Tuesday," Oct. 24, 1929, the day of the Wall Street crash.

Its first foreign victims were in Latin America, which was dependent on the American market for selling raw materials. Europe was not affected immediately; American loans and investments there dwindled only slowly. By 1931, however, the flow of capital had virtually ceased, and direct investment dried up in the following year. Worse still, to pay their own debts, Americans repatriated huge sums of money. Germany, Austria, and Britain were the hardest hit. Between the end of May and the middle of July in 1931, the German central bank, the Reichsbank, lost $2 billion in gold and foreign currency. To compound Europe's problems, on June 17, 1930, the United States enacted the protective Smoot-Hawley Tariff Act, increasing the average import duty level to about 50 percent.

The combined results were catastrophic. Highly respected banks failed, first among them the great Kreditanstalt of Vienna, which collapsed in May 1931. The Bank of England, at that time, was losing gold at the rate of £2.5 million a day. Everywhere, industrial production fell: by 40 percent in Germany, 14 percent in Britain, and 29 percent in France.

On June 20, 1931, U.S. President Herbert Hoover announced a year's moratorium on all government debts.

When it expired in June 1932, the secretary of state, Henry Stimson, proposed a year's extension, but Hoover refused. The Europeans had meanwhile agreed to cancel their claims on German reparations but not to ratify this decision unless the United States wrote off their war debts. The Americans, seeing this as a European conspiracy, demanded continued payment. At this, all the European nations except Finland dug their heels in, exacerbating U.S. isolationism and making a global solution of the crisis still more unlikely.

In June 1933, nevertheless, a World Economic Conference met in London. Hoover's successor as president, Franklin D. Roosevelt, made his secretary of state, Cordell Hull, the head of the U.S. delegation. Hull was a free-trader, but in July 1933 Roosevelt sent a message to the conference insisting that its main concern must be monetary exchanges, and in January 1934 the United States passed the Johnson Act, forbidding even private loans to countries that had not paid their war debts.

So there was no global solution: it was every man for himself. Some European countries—Germany in 1930–32, France until 1936—responded by deflation; they maintained the external value of their currencies but reduced their export prices by cutting wages and costs. The result was social unrest. In Germany, Chancellor Brüning's 1930 decrees of the dissolution of the Reichstag and government by presidential order led to 107 Nazis and 77 communists being elected to Parliament that September. In France, Pierre Laval's decrees led to the 1936 success of the left-wing Popular Front.

Other countries took to devaluation, leaving the gold standard to which Belgium, France, Italy, the Netherlands, and Switzerland still clung from 1931 to 1935. Britain devalued in September 1931, the United States in April 1933, and France in September 1936. This had the effect of making exports cheaper, but since it made imports more expensive it worked only if they could be discouraged by high tariffs (as in the United States) or if the country in question had access to cheap raw materials (as in Britain's system of imperial preference).

A third option was to impose exchange controls to cut the economy off from world markets. This was the solution adopted by Germany in 1932 and by most of central Europe and the Balkans. It had the effect of creating German hegemony, since those central European and Balkan countries that needed to sell to the large German market were unable to repatriate their earnings and had to buy German goods. In 1932 Germany saw exchange controls and their effects as a temporary expedient. For Adolf Hitler and the Nazi party, however, they became part of a settled and sinister policy.

The Trappings of Dictatorship

Totalitarian dictatorship was a phenomenon first localized in 20th-century Europe. A number of developments made it possible. Since the 19th century the machine gun had greatly facilitated drastic crowd control. Public address systems, radio, and, later, television made it easy for an individual orator to move a multitude. Films offered new scope for propaganda. Psychology and pharmaceuticals lent themselves to brainwashing. Miniature cameras and electronic listening devices simplified surveillance. Heavy artillery, aircraft, and fast armoured vehicles provided the means for waging a blitzkrieg, or "lightning war." Bullies and brutality, of course, there had always been.

The European dictatorships were far from identical. They differed in their historical roots, their social contexts, their ideologies, and their trappings. But they bore

Dictatorship

Dictatorship is a form of government in which one person or a small group possesses absolute power without effective constitutional limitations. The term dictatorship comes from the Latin title dictator, which in the Roman Republic designated a temporary magistrate who was granted extraordinary powers in order to deal with state crises. Modern dictators, however, resemble ancient tyrants rather than ancient dictators. Ancient philosophers' descriptions of the tyrannies of Greece and Sicily go far toward characterizing modern dictatorships. Dictators usually resort to force or fraud to gain despotic political power, which they maintain through the use of intimidation, terror, and the suppression of basic civil liberties. They may also employ techniques of mass propaganda in order to sustain their public support.

The communist and fascist dictatorships that arose in various technologically advanced countries in the first half of the 20th century were distinctively different from the authoritarian regimes of 19th-century Latin America or the postcolonial dictatorships of Africa and Asia. Nazi Germany under Adolf Hitler and the Soviet Union under Joseph Stalin were the leading examples of such modern totalitarian dictatorships. The crucial elements of both were the identification of the state with a single mass party and of the party with its charismatic leader, the use of an official ideology to legitimize and maintain the regime, the use of terror and propaganda to suppress dissent and stifle opposition, and the use of modern science and technology to control the economy and individual behaviour. Soviet-type communist dictatorships arose in central and eastern Europe, China, and other countries in the wake of World War II, though most of them (as well as the Soviet Union itself) had collapsed by the last decade of the 20th century.

a family resemblance. Political analysis may underplay it; to their victims, it was all too obvious.

Europe's first practical dictatorship was established in Russia by the Bolshevik Revolution of 1917. Its emblem, the hammer and sickle, represented physical labour in factory or field; there was no symbol for the scientist, the statesman, or the scholar. The aims of the revolution—liquidating the capitalist economic system, increasing public wealth, raising the material and cultural standard of working people—had wide appeal. But in its concern to industrialize and modernize a huge, backward union of republics with a long cultural legacy of tsarist domination that had been replaced by a centralizing socialist ideology, it relied on a one-party state, heavy censorship, the suppression of individual liberty, and the murder of awkward opponents. Theoretically, it foresaw "the withering away of the state." For the time being, it embodied "the dictatorship of the proletariat"—or rather of a single leader, first Vladimir Ilich Lenin, then Joseph Stalin.

Two years after the Russian Revolution, in 1919, Benito Mussolini founded the Fascist Party in Italy. Its emblem, the fasces (a bundle of rods with an axe in the centre), was a symbol of state power adopted from ancient Rome. Explicitly anticommunist, it was as opposed to the withering away of the state as it was to individualistic liberalism. "For the Fascist," wrote Mussolini, "everything is the State." His own regime, partially established in 1924 and completed in 1928–29, had its bullyboys and castor-oil torture, its murders and aggressive wars. But, for sociological and cultural, as well as political, reasons, it was both less systematic and less brutal than some other European dictatorships. Italy had a long tradition of regional diversity that resisted uniformity, and Italian society was permeated—in complex, sometimes contradictory ways—by the ubiquitous influence of the Roman Catholic Church.

Benito Mussolini, Italian dictator and founder of Italy's Fascist Party. Topical Press Agency/Hulton Archive/Getty Images

Forms of fascism took root in other Latin countries. In Spain in 1923 General Miguel Primo de Rivera seized power with the approval of the king. He dissolved Parliament, imprisoned democratic leaders, suspended trial by jury, censored the press, and placed the country under martial law. He tried to establish a fully fascist regime based on "Country, Religion, and the Monarchy," but he met resistance from students and workers and abandoned the attempt in 1925, although he remained prime minister until 1930. In 1931 a republic was proclaimed, headed by a provisional government of republicans and socialists.

Meanwhile, in neighbouring Portugal, António de Oliveira Salazar, a professor of economics, had been made finance minister after a military coup d'état in 1926; and, although he had resigned soon afterward, he had been recalled in 1928. After reorganizing the Portuguese budget, in 1932 he was offered the premiership. His conception of what he called the "Estado Novo," or "New State," was corporatist and fascist. Its authoritarian constitution, endorsed by plebiscite in 1933, allowed only one political party, the National Union (União Nacional).

In 1936 a general election in Spain gave a clear majority to the left. On May 10, Manuel Azaña, the Popular Front leader, was elected president, but two months later a group of army officers led by General Francisco Franco staged a fascist revolt. Supplied with arms, air power, and "volunteers" by Mussolini and Hitler, Franco's forces won the ensuing Spanish Civil War—although it dragged on until 1939, when the U.S.S.R. finally cut off the aid it had given to the Republican government. The French and British governments pursued a policy of nonintervention, although an International Brigade of private volunteers fought alongside the Republicans. One significant feature of the Spanish Civil War was its use by Nazi pilots as a training ground for the dive-bombing tactics they later employed in World War II.

Nazi Germany, in fact, was Europe's most elaborately developed dictatorship. Characteristically, Hitler took great care with the design of its emblem, a black swastika in a white circle on a red background; as iconography, it has long survived its regime. The swastika, originally the obverse of the Nazi version, was an Eastern mystic symbol brought into Europe in the 6th century and reappropriated. Nazi ideology differed from fascism in at least two respects. It regarded the state as a means, rather than an end in itself, and the end it envisaged was the supremacy of what Hitler believed to be "the Aryan master race." The final result—Hitler's so-called Final Solution—was the systematic slaughter of at least six million Jews and millions of others whom the Nazis referred to as inferior peoples.

Nazi leader Adolf Hitler, front right, *wears on his arm the party's swastika symbol, an emblem that came to represent all the atrocities and horrors of World War II.* Hulton Archive/Getty Images

Born in Austria, Hitler had fought in World War I in the Bavarian infantry, twice winning the Iron Cross. In September 1919, six months after Mussolini founded the Italian Fascist Party, Hitler joined a German nationalist group that took the name of National Socialist German Workers' Party (Nationalsozialistische Deutsche Arbeiterpartei), nicknamed "Nazi," a truncation of Nationalsozialistische. Its policies included anti-Semitism and fierce opposition to the Treaty of Versailles. After his abortive Munich coup in 1923, Hitler was sentenced to five years' imprisonment, of which he served nine months. While in prison, he wrote his autobiographical manifesto, *Mein Kampf*.

In 1930, with 107 seats, the Nazis became the second largest party in Parliament. On Jan. 30, 1933, after three ineffectual chancellors, President Paul von Hindenburg appointed Hitler to the post, believing that the vice-chancellor, Franz von Papen, would counterbalance any Nazi excess.

Four weeks later the Reichstag building in Berlin was gutted by a fire probably started by a foolish young Dutch communist, but certainly exploited by the Nazis as evidence of an alleged communist plot. Hitler used the excuse to enact decrees that gave his party totalitarian powers. In the following June he eliminated most potential rivals, and when Hindenburg died on Aug. 2, 1934, Hitler was proclaimed *Führer*, or leader of the German Reich.

Hitler's foreign policy triumphs followed: the reoccupation of the Rhineland and the alliance with Mussolini in 1936; the *Anschluss* ("union") with Austria and the occupation of Czechoslovakia in 1938–39; and in 1939 the German-Soviet Nonaggression Pact. Until Hitler's invasion of Poland in September of that year, it sometimes seemed as if Europe's democracies could only look on, prevaricate, and tremble.

The Phony Peace

The early months of World War II, marked by no major hostilities, came to be known as "the Phony War." The 1930s, marked by war in Spain and the fear of war throughout Europe, might as aptly be called "the Phony Peace."

Economically, that decade saw a gradual revival of prosperity in most of Europe. For the middle classes in some countries, indeed, it was a slightly hollow golden age. Many could still afford servants, often drawn from the ranks of unmarried girls from poor families with few skills to sell. "Ribbon development" of suburbs was providing new houses on the cleaner outskirts of cities, served by expanding urban transport systems. Every suburb had one or more palatial cinemas showing talking pictures, some of them even in colour. Gramophones and records were improving their quality, radio sets were growing more compact and versatile, and, toward the end of the decade, television began. Cheaper automobiles were appearing on the market, telephones and refrigerators were becoming general, and some homes began to boast washing machines. Air travel was still a rarity but was no longer unheard of. The cheap franc made France a playground for tourists from countries with harder currencies.

For those less privileged, daily life was far less benign. Deference was still deeply ingrained in European society. The humbler classes dressed differently, ate differently, and spoke differently; they even walked and stood differently. They certainly had different homes, often lacking a bathroom or an indoor lavatory. Unemployment was still widespread. In Britain, in the Tyneside town of Jarrow, starting point of the 1936 protest march to Westminster, almost 70 percent of the work force was out of a job. Those in work still faced long hours; dirty, noisy, and dangerous conditions; and monotonous, repetitive assembly-line tasks. Some of the workers were women, but, despite their "liberation" during World War I, many had returned to domesticity, which to some seemed drudgery. Young people had yet to acquire the affluence that later gave them such independence and self-assurance as an economic and cultural group.

Beneath the placid surface, moreover, there were undercurrents of unease. On the right, especially in France and Germany, there was still much fear of bolshevism. Some, for this reason, saw merits in Mussolini, while a few were attracted by Hitler. On the left, conversely, many admired the U.S.S.R.—although some, such as the French writer André Gide, changed their minds when they had seen it. But left, right, and centre in most of the democracies had one thing in common, though they differed radically about how to deal with it. What they shared was a growing fear of war. Having fought and won, with American help, "the war to end war," were they now to face the same peril all over again?

This fear became acute toward the end of the decade, as Hitler's ambitions grew more and more plain. But underlying it was a broader, deeper, and less specific disquiet, especially in continental Europe.

In 1918 the German philosopher of history Oswald Spengler published *Der Untergang des Abendlandes*, translated in 1926–28 as *The Decline of the West*. In 1920 the French geographer Albert Demangeon produced *The Decline of Europe*. In 1927 Julien Benda published his classic study *The Great Betrayal*, and in 1930 José Ortega y Gasset produced *The Revolt of the Masses*. All these works—and many others—evoked what the Dutch historian Johan Huizinga called, in the title of a book published in 1928, *The Crisis of Civilisation*. That same year, coincidentally, saw René Guenon's *The Crisis of the Modern World*. Similar concerns were voiced in Britain almost a decade later, when the French-born Roman Catholic writer Hilaire Belloc published *The Crisis of Our Civilization*.

Many such writers were pessimistic. Paul Valéry, in *Glimpses of the Modern World* (1931), warned Europeans against abandoning intellectual discipline and embracing chauvinism, fanaticism, and war. Thomas Mann, in *Warning Europe* (1938), asked: "Has European humanism become incapable of resurrection?" "For the moment," wrote Carl J. Burckhardt, "it…seems that the world will be destroyed before one of the great nations of Europe gives up its demand for supremacy."

At Munich in September 1938 the British prime minister Neville Chamberlain and his French counterpart Édouard Daladier bought time with "appeasement"—betraying Czechoslovakia and handing the Sudetenland to Hitler. Millions cheered the empty pledge they brought back with them: "Peace for our time." Within 11 months Hitler had invaded Poland and World War II had begun.

THE BLAST OF WORLD WAR II

World War II was the most destructive war in history. Estimates of those killed vary from 35 million to 60 million. The total for Europe alone was 15 million to 20 million—more than twice as many as in World War I. At least 6 million Jewish men, women, and children, and millions of others, were systematically murdered by Hitler's regime. Nor were the Germans themselves spared. By 1945, in a population of some 70 million, there were 7 million more German women than men.

One after another, most of the countries in continental Europe had been invaded and occupied: Austria, Czechoslovakia, Albania, Poland, Finland, Denmark, Norway, Belgium, the Netherlands, Luxembourg, France, Lithuania, Latvia, Estonia, Romania, Bulgaria, Hungary,

Greece, Yugoslavia, and the U.S.S.R. and then, when the tide turned, Italy and Germany. Many countries had been fought over twice.

The resulting devastation had turned much of Europe into a moonscape: cities laid waste or consumed by firestorms, the countryside charred and blackened, roads pitted with shell holes or bomb craters, railways out of action, bridges destroyed or truncated, harbours filled with sunken, listing ships. "Berlin," said General Lucius D. Clay, the deputy military governor in the U.S. zone of postwar Germany, "was like a city of the dead."

Between 1939 and 1945, moreover, at least 60 million European civilians had been uprooted from their homes; 27 million had left their own countries or been driven out by force. Four and a half million had been deported by the Nazis for forced labour; many thousands more had been sent to Siberia by the Russians. When the war ended, 2.5 million Poles and Czechs were transferred to the U.S.S.R., and more than 12 million Germans fled or were expelled from eastern Europe. At one period in 1945, 40,000 refugees a week poured into northwestern Germany.

Death, destruction, and mass displacements—all had demonstrated how fragile and vulnerable Europe's proud nations had become. In most earlier conflicts the state's defenses had been its frontiers or its front line: its armies had been a carapace protecting the civilians within. Now, even more than in World War I, this was no longer so. Air raids, rockets, mass conscription, blitzkrieg invasion, commando raids, parachute drops, Resistance sabotage, and guerrilla warfare had put everyone, as the phrase went, "in the front line." More accurately, national frontiers had shown how flimsy they were, and the "front line" metaphor had lost its force. Even the distinction between civilians and soldiers had become blurred. Civilians had fought in Resistance circuits—and been shot, sometimes as hostages, and when the Allies or the Axis practiced area bombing, civilians were the main victims. The most extreme instances were the atomic bombs dropped on Hiroshima and Nagasaki in Japan. They not only ignored the civilian-military distinction; they utterly transformed the nature of war.

Hitler's death camps, likewise, made World War II unique. The appalling product of spurious science, evil fanaticism, blind bureaucratic obedience, sadistic perversion, and pedantic callousness, they left an unhealing wound. They reminded humanity of the depths to which human beings can sink and of the vital need to expunge racism of all kinds—including the reflex, understandable at the time, of regarding the Germans as solely capable of committing Nazi-type crimes.

The Nürnberg trials were a further unique feature of World War II (although war trials were written into the treaties following World War I). By arraigning and punishing major surviving Nazi leaders, they undoubtedly supplied a salutary form of catharsis, if nothing else. They proved beyond a doubt the wickedness of Hitler's regime; at one point, when films of the death camps were shown, they actually sickened and shamed the defendants. In some eyes, however, the trials were tainted. Although scrupulously conducted, they smacked slightly of show trials, with the victorious Allies playing both prosecutor and judge. Given the purges of millions under Stalin, the participation of Soviet judges seemed especially hypocritical. The charges included not only war crimes, of which many of the accused were manifestly guilty, but also "waging aggressive war"—a novel addition to the statute book. Finally, a number of war criminals certainly slipped through the Nürnberg net. The overall intention, however, was surely honourable: to establish once and for all that international affairs were not immune from ethical

Twenty-one of the 24 former Nazi leaders charged with war crimes for their roles in German aggression and genocide wait in the dock for their final sentences during the Nürnberg trials. Archive Photos/Getty Images

considerations and that international law—unlike the League of Nations—was growing teeth.

In two further respects, World War II left a lasting mark on Europe. The first and most obvious was its division between East and West. Both U.S. and Soviet troops, from opposite directions, had helped to liberate Europe, and on April 25, 1945, they met on the Elbe River. They toasted each other and posed for the photographers; then the Soviets dug themselves into new defensive positions, still facing west.

It was not a confrontation, but it was symbolic. Stalin had long made clear that he sought to recover the three Baltic republics of Latvia, Lithuania, and Estonia, as well as the part of Poland that the Poles had seized after Versailles. He also expected a free hand in exerting influence on the rest of eastern Europe. At a meeting in Moscow in October 1944, Churchill had largely conceded this principle, proposing 90 percent Soviet influence in Romania, 90 percent British influence in Greece, 75 percent Soviet influence in Bulgaria, and a 50–50 split in Yugoslavia and Hungary. Cynical as this might seem, it was a tacit recognition of strategic and military facts. Similar considerations determined the East-West zonal division of Germany, which endured in the form of two German republics until their reunification in October 1990.

The fact that the U.S.S.R. and the United States now faced each other in Europe along the so-called "Iron Curtain" denounced by Churchill in his Fulton, Mo., speech on March 5, 1946, dramatized Europe's final legacy from World War II. This was a drastic reduction in wealth, status, and power.

In financial terms, World War II had cost more than the combined total of all European wars since the Middle Ages. Even Britain, which had been spared invasion, had been transformed from the world's biggest creditor to the world's biggest debtor, and much of continental Europe was obliged to continue living on credit and aid. Economically, all Europe's once great powers were dwarfed by the world's superpowers. Their status was diminished still further when their remaining colonies were freed.

CHAPTER 7

Postwar Europe, 1945 to the Present

International planning for peace after World War II took place on a world scale. Within five years, in an extraordinary burst of energy and imagination, statesmen endowed the world with almost all its existing network of global institutions: the United Nations (UN), the Food and Agriculture Organization (FAO), the International Monetary Fund (the IMF), the International Bank for Reconstruction and Development (the IBRD, or World Bank), the United Nations Educational, Scientific, and Cultural Organization (UNESCO), the United Nations International Children's Emergency Fund (UNICEF), the International Court of Justice, the General Agreement on Tariffs and Trade (GATT), the International Refugee Organization (IRO), the World Health Organization (WHO), the United Nations Relief and Works Agency (UNRWA), and the International Confederation of Free Trade Unions (ICFTU). Some of these, especially the United Nations, were to reveal limitations. But they embodied serious efforts to replace outdated national and bilateral diplomacy with permanent multilateral institutions.

Domestically, many people's first instinct after World War II was to return to normal: to restore law and order after the euphoric anarchy of liberation; to repatriate prisoners and demobilize soldiers; to reopen the bombed Teatro alla Scala, Milan, and have Arturo Toscanini conduct there again; and to bring back long dresses with Christian Dior's "New Look." At the same time, however, there was deep eagerness for change. Even more than World War I, World War II had been a democratic war, fought against dictatorship as much as against aggression. Like many wars, it had brought forth military and other leaders from the rank and file. For many the aim was to inaugurate a new and more just society within nation-states that were pledged to work together for peace. "From Resistance to Revolution" was the masthead slogan of *Combat*, the left-wing French Resistance newspaper founded in 1941 but after the war edited as a Paris daily by the novelist Albert Camus. The words could well have been endorsed by others, especially the radical Action Party in Italy and many socialists there and elsewhere.

No less innovative, if less radical, were the Christian Democrat parties springing up or being revived: the Christian Democrats in Italy, the Christian Democratic Union in Germany, the Dutch People's Movement in the Netherlands, the Popular Republican Movement in France. At that time, most Roman Catholic parties had a more left-of-centre tone than was later the case.

Britain had no Christian Democrat party, and its Labour Party had less in common with continental socialist ideology than with nonconformism and the trade union movement. Yet the British people shared the general impatience for change, as they showed when they voted in large numbers for Labour in the 1945 general election, roundly defeating the Conservatives under Winston Churchill, who had led the country so memorably during the war.

In its election manifesto, the Labour Party proposed a program of nationalization of the Bank of England, of fuel and power, of iron and steel, and of inland waterways. It endorsed the Education Act already steered through by the moderate Conservative R. A. Butler. It proposed a national health service and a social security system, and it called for physical controls to allocate raw materials, limit food prices, provide new homes, and direct the location of industry.

Similar reforms were envisaged throughout western Europe. They embraced more equality, fairer shares, and better social conditions—full employment, higher wages, fairer taxes, more trade union rights, antitrust provisions, government-funded social security, and (where necessary) land reform. Such measures also implied far more central control of the economy.

"Planning" was now a common objective. In Italy it was the responsibility of the Institute of Industrial Reconstruction. In Britain the government maintained the machinery of statutory controls that it had used in wartime. In Germany the banks played a major role in forecasting, steering, and assisting investment. But in France it was the extraordinary Jean Monnet who made planning a concerted national effort rather than a set of directives from above.

Between the wars Monnet had been deputy secretary-general of the League of Nations, a private banker, and a negotiator for the French government. In the United States during World War II he had helped to spur Roosevelt's Victory Program of aircraft for the Allies. Subsequently, in Algiers, he had helped to reconcile General Charles de Gaulle with his American-backed rival General Henri Giraud. It was to de Gaulle, who shortly became premier of France, that Monnet proposed a planning commissariat, attached only to the prime minister's office and bringing together for the first time in France industrialists, labour unions, and senior civil servants to discuss production targets, supplies, bottlenecks, and urgent action in key sectors of the economy. Revolutionary at the time, the plan was highly successful and was soon imitated elsewhere.

National planning alone, however, could not solve Europe's problems. Joint action was needed, as was help from the United States. In 1947, two years after the end of the war, many Europeans were still leading a Spartan existence. Everywhere, food continued to be rationed. Dimmed lights, brownouts, and power cuts were still common. A hard winter and waves of strikes added to the general misery. Underlying it was the stark fact that the countries of Europe were in serious financial trouble.

They had long been living on handouts. By October 1945 the United States had advanced some $46 billion in nonrepayable "lend-lease" loans. When the war ended, so did lend-lease—to be replaced by huge stopgap loans on ordinary terms. Britain received $3.75 billion, but only on condition that it make sterling freely convertible. As soon as it did, there was a run on the pound. The entire loan, it was reckoned, would have melted away in two and a half months if Britain had not suspended convertibility. As it was, a third of the credit was wiped out by price increases in the United States.

Britain, in fact, was overextended. In 1946 it had spent $60 million to help feed the German people, and it still had one and a half million troops trying to police the globe. Already, on Feb. 21, 1947, Britain had warned the United States that it would soon have to cancel economic and military aid to Greece and Turkey. It was this message that triggered a rescue operation for the whole of western Europe.

THE UNITED STATES TO THE RESCUE

Greece and Turkey, in the Cold War conditions of 1947, were strategically vital and highly vulnerable Western outposts on the southern flank of the U.S.S.R. and its satellite states. Turkey was especially exposed. In Greece, the mainly communist National Liberation Front (EAM) had failed in its violent bid for power, but guerrilla units were still fighting in the Pindus Mountains and the Peloponnese, and the Greek economy was near collapse.

The news that Britain was to pull out of the Balkans horrified Washington. Dean Acheson, the under secretary of state, called the British messages "shockers." With George Marshall, the secretary of state, he lost no time in tackling the problem. After conferring with them, President Harry S. Truman called in the congressional leaders—and managed to win to his cause the influential Republican senator Arthur H. Vandenberg, theretofore a notorious isolationist. With his support secured, Acheson felt able to quote to the British ambassador the motto of the Seabees: "We do the difficult at once; the impossible takes a little longer."

On March 12, 1947, less than three weeks after Britain's plea for help, Truman announced to Congress what came to be called the Truman Doctrine: U.S. support for free peoples against armed subjugation, primarily through economic and financial aid. By May 22 he had been empowered to sign the Greek-Turkish Aid Act.

Reports from Europe, however, showed that other countries were equally in need of American help. On June 5, 1947, Marshall gave a 10-minute commencement address at Harvard University and thereby launched the Marshall Plan. This and the Truman Doctrine, Truman remarked later, were "two halves of the same walnut." Marshall told his audience,

> *Europe's requirements for the next three or four years of foreign food and other essential products are so much greater than her present ability to pay that she must have substantial additional help.*

Without it, the economic, social, and political outcome could be "very grave":

> *Aside from the demoralizing effect on the world at large and the possibilities of disturbances arising as a result of the desperation of the people concerned, the consequences to the economy of the United States should be apparent to all. It is logical that the United States should do whatever it is able to do to assist in the return of normal economic health in the world, without which there can be no political stability and no assured peace.*

Marshall added three conditions. First, aid must be systematic, not piecemeal. Second, the countries of Europe must work out their needs and plans together. Third, public opinion must endorse the policy.

Hearing the news of Marshall's speech and a commentary by a specially briefed British journalist, British foreign secretary Ernest Bevin "grabbed the proposals," as he said later, "with both hands." With French foreign minister Georges Bidault, he invited their colleague from the U.S.S.R., Vyacheslav Mikhaylovich Molotov, to join in a collective response to the Marshall offer. Molotov refused, attacking the plan as a violation of sovereignty. Later the U.S.S.R. prevented Czechoslovakia from taking it up.

So it was that the Marshall Plan was confined to western Europe. On July 12, 1947, the representatives of 16 nations met in Paris: Austria, Belgium, Denmark, France, Greece, Iceland, Ireland, Italy, Luxembourg, the Netherlands, Norway, Portugal, Sweden, Switzerland, Turkey, and the United Kingdom. Four days later they set up a temporary Committee of European Economic Co-operation under Sir Oliver Franks. By the third week in September it had produced a draft four-year recovery plan, which was subsequently much revised. Under powerful U.S. pressure, the Europeans reluctantly agreed to establish a permanent body in place of the temporary committee. It was finally inaugurated as the Organisation for European Economic Co-operation (OEEC) on April 16, 1948.

By then the U.S. Congress had approved the European Recovery Program, and Truman had appointed Paul Hoffman to administer it. Within two weeks of his appointment, the freighter *John H. Quick* sailed for Europe from Galveston, Texas, with 9,000 tons of wheat. It was the first of many, carrying every kind of commodity from spiced ham to tractors, from powdered eggs to machine tools. Within Europe, Marshall aid made possible some spectacular projects. They ranged from land reclamation in Italy and the Netherlands to a dam in Austria harnessing water power from melting glaciers. In all, the European Recovery Program brought Europe grants and credits totaling $13.15 billion—5 percent of the national income of the United States. At the same time, private relief parcels amounted to over $500 million—more than $3, on average, from every American man, woman, and child.

The United States' timely generosity saved Europe from imminent economic ruin and laid firm foundations for later economic growth. By 1950 trade within western Europe had recovered to its prewar volume, two years ahead of expectations, and by 1951 European industrial output was 43 percent greater than before the war. U.S. insistence on a coordinated approach to recovery supplied the incentive and the institutions for permanent mutual consultations; in the process, the OEEC gradually reduced the quantitative and monetary barriers that had hamstrung intra-European trade. It failed, however, to remove tariffs. U.S. pressure for a European customs union eventually came to nothing; although willing to consult and cooperate, Europeans were not yet ready for economic integration, still less political union.

This made difficult a relationship of equals between European countries and the United States. But, short of that, the Marshall Plan did lead to much closer transatlantic ties. Under W. Averell Harriman, its Paris-based chief representative, U.S. experts worked throughout Europe. "They swooped down here," said one German businessman, "like birds on a field." By 1952 the U.S. embassy in Paris was responsible for 2,500 U.S. officials, plus 5,000 family members. Within a decade, 40,000 private American businessmen had settled in Europe, working for 3,000 American companies, whose European investments had quadrupled in that time.

War and peace had brought Europeans and Americans closer together than at any time since the mass migrations from the Old World to the New. Their mutual relations were complex and ambivalent: a blend of European gratitude, envy, and slight resentment combined with American impatience, fascination, and missionary zeal. As time went on, some Europeans complained of "Americanization"; what this often meant was merely that innovations had reached the United States first. But, for all their differences, Americans and western Europeans had one great common commitment—to a free and democratic way of life, which in eastern Europe had been progressively suppressed.

A Climate of Fear

By the time that Roosevelt, Churchill, and Stalin had held their Yalta Conference in February 1945, Europe was already divided between East and West; Yalta, therefore, was not to blame for the division. On the contrary, it could

British Prime Minister Winston Churchill, left, *U.S. Pres. Franklin Roosevelt,* centre, *and Soviet Premier Joseph Stalin meet at Yalta in 1945 to discuss the defeat and postwar division of Germany.* Herbert/Hulton Archive/Getty Images

in theory have reunited Europe, since all three powers had pledged themselves to help any liberated or former Axis satellite state form an interim government broadly representing all democratic elements, followed as soon as possible by free elections. The Western Allies kept their Yalta promise; Stalin did not.

One after another, Stalin subjected all but two of the eastern European countries to a similar takeover process. It was described frankly, in retrospect, in a textbook published between 1948 and 1950 by the Communist Party of Czechoslovakia: *How Parliament Can Play a Revolutionary Part in the Transition to Socialism and the Role of the Popular Masses*. First, communist ministers were imposed upon the existing coalition government, if possible in key posts such as the Ministry of the Interior. Then, the party gradually established or infiltrated power centres outside parliament—for instance, by arming the proletariat, setting up action committees, or expanding the secret police. This would create "a pincer movement operating from above and below." The end product was an antidemocratic coup. Even if the bourgeoisie still retained some support in the country, a short period of "people's democratic government" would soon achieve "the disintegration of the political army upon which the bourgeoisie could formerly count."

The exceptions to this routine were Finland and Yugoslavia, each favoured by geography and supported by a powerful patriotic army. While both, in 1945, acquired left-wing, Marxist governments, both felt strong enough to resist domination by the U.S.S.R. This was not the case in Albania, Poland, Bulgaria, Romania, Hungary, and Czechoslovakia—all of which succumbed to the "pincer movement" or "salami tactics" of the Czechoslovak textbook.

In Albania there was not even a preliminary coalition. At the first postwar elections in December 1945, voters faced a single list of candidates without opposition. Not surprisingly, it won an 86 percent majority. Subsequent referenda, designed to sidestep the high rate of illiteracy, gave voters a ball to drop into a "Yes" or a "No" slot. Through the former, it fell silently into a sack; through the latter, it rattled into a can.

In Poland the postwar coalition included a minority of members returned from wartime exile in London, but a majority were their rivals, backed by the U.S.S.R., who held such key positions as the Ministry of Public Security and resorted to censorship, threats, and murder against the bourgeois parties and the press. The eventual election, held under a reign of terror in January 1947, gave a landslide victory to left-wing socialists and communists. Already in the previous September they had agreed with Stalin and Molotov on the composition of the future government.

In Bulgaria's coalition government, formed in 1944, communists held the Ministries of Interior and Justice. Purges, intimidation, and the imprisonment of opposition leaders made the eventual election a mockery. When Georgi Dimitrov (who had been one of the defendants in the German Reichstag fire trial) became prime minister of a fresh coalition in 1946, his Cabinet included nine communist ministers, making the coalition a mere façade.

In Romania in 1945, the U.S.S.R. insisted that King Michael, who had set up a coalition government, should accept in it communist ministers of the interior and of justice. In the subsequent 1946 election campaign, the communists broke up rival meetings, persuaded printers to boycott opposition literature, and imprisoned or killed political opponents.

In Hungary the 1944 coalition included only two communist ministers, and in the 1945 election the moderate-liberal Smallholders' Party led the poll. The communists threatened to quit the government, leaving it as a minority, unless they were given the Ministry of the Interior. They organized demonstrations and insisted on the dismissal of 22 Smallholders' representatives. In December 1946 the communist ministers of defense and of the interior made widespread arrests. In August 1947, 35 percent of the electorate still voted for the opposition, closely linked with the Roman Catholic Church. However, in 1949, after the arrest and imprisonment of József Cardinal Mindszenty, the government staged a single-list election and claimed 90 percent of the votes.

In Czechoslovakia the 1945 coalition provisional government had communists at the Ministries of the Interior, Education, Agriculture, and Information. In the 1946 election of a Constituent Assembly the communists and their Social Democratic allies held a slender majority, and for two years the country prospered. But, as the 1948 election approached, the communists prepared for a takeover. The minister of the interior dismissed eight noncommunist police commanders in Prague, replacing them with party men. In the ensuing protest in the Cabinet, the non-Marxist ministers resigned, but the Social Democrats unexpectedly remained and kept the government in place. When the ex-ministers tried to return, they were ejected. The communists, assured of backing by the U.S.S.R., staged strikes, armed workers' rallies, and a violent putsch. Their most illustrious victim was Jan Masaryk, the foreign minister, son of the republic's founder, who died on the night of March 9, 1948. Czechoslovak democracy died with him—and would not be resurrected for 40 years.

With communist ministers in the postwar governments of Belgium, France, and Italy, and with communists fomenting political strikes, some feared similar takeovers in the West. Germany, however, was the scene of the sharpest clash. For several years, by a leapfrog process of move and countermove, the eastern and western occupation zones of Germany had gradually been solidifying into separate entities. When in June 1948 the Western authorities issued a new western deutsche mark, the U.S.S.R. retaliated by imposing a land blockade on Berlin, which was jointly administered by the four occupation powers but was physically an enclave within the Soviet zone. The West responded with a massive 11-month airlift of food, goods, and raw materials. Meanwhile, 12 Western countries—Belgium, Britain, Canada, Denmark, France, Iceland, Italy, Luxembourg, the Netherlands, Norway, Portugal, and the United States—negotiated and signed on April 4, 1949, the North Atlantic Treaty, agreeing "that an armed attack against one or more of them...shall be considered an attack against them all." Almost immediately, the U.S.S.R. called off the Berlin blockade.

Within a few weeks, Germany was formally divided into two rival republics. The Cold War had reached a climax. Western Europe had drawn even closer to the United States.

AFFLUENCE AND ITS UNDERSIDE

The West German currency reform that produced the western deutsche mark was a courageous act. It exchanged one deutsche mark for 10 obsolete reichsmarks; later the rate was slightly reduced. In one respect, the result was similar to that of Weimar's hyperinflation—paper savings were suddenly devalued. This time, however, there was a limit to any losses. What was more, quite small quantities of the new currency would actually buy goods. When Ludwig Erhard, the economic director who had undertaken the reform, also dismantled price and other controls, the scene was set for the so-called *Wirtschaftswunder*, the German "economic miracle," fueled by freedom and competition and the energy they released.

By 1950 West Germany's gross national product had caught up with the 1936 figure. Between 1950 and 1955 the national income rose by 12 percent a year, while exports grew even faster. From a small deficit in 1950, gold and foreign currency reserves increased to nearly 13 billion deutsche marks by 1955, while unemployment fell from 2.5 million to 900,000. Per capita income nearly doubled. New homes were built at the rate of 500,000 a year. By 1955 West Germany had more than 100,000 television sets. Bombed cities had been rebuilt. Every other family seemed to possess a Volkswagen "beetle" car.

West Germany's was not the only economic miracle. France, spurred by the bright young graduates of *grandes écoles* like the Polytechnique, was modernizing rapidly—electrifying railways, launching new power projects, discovering natural gas, building nuclear reactors, mechanizing coal mines, and designing the Caravelle jet airplane. In 1948 France's total output had been only just above the 1936 level. By 1955 it was half again as high. Between 1955 and 1958 French productivity increased by 8 percent a year, faster than anywhere else in Europe.

Italy, however, was not to be left behind. With a comparatively low starting point, plentiful labour, and new discoveries of oil and, especially, natural gas, it was able to increase the gross national product by 32.9 percent between 1950 and 1954. In Italian industry between 1950 and 1958, the average annual growth rate was 9 percent. As in West Germany, the transformation was visible: better clothes, smarter shop fronts, higher meat consumption, and bicycles replaced by motor scooters and later by small cars.

In Britain, although there was no economic miracle, there were industrial success stories in chemicals, quality cars, nuclear energy, and aviation. It was a British airline that in 1952 inaugurated the world's first purely jet airline service. By the end of the decade, Heathrow in London was the busiest airport in the world.

By 1955 all western European countries were producing more than in the 1930s. Abroad, from 1952 onward, western Europe was earning more than it spent. Between 1950 and 1955, average productivity in Europe increased by 26 percent. Although British Prime Minister Harold Macmillan was both misunderstood and mocked when he made the remark, he had some justification for telling an audience on July 20, 1957: "Most of our people have never had it so good."

The benefits, for ordinary Europeans, took many forms. There was easier access to higher education and cheaper mass travel. There was more varied food and better health, preserved by better medicine. There were new synthetic materials, more plentiful housing, and wider automobile ownership. There were stereophonic recordings, colour television, high-fidelity audio equipment, and cheap paperback editions of serious books. There were new, more classless eating-houses, pedestrian precincts, supermarkets, and shopping malls. What its critics called "Americanization" had arrived.

But affluence had a downside, in Europe as elsewhere. It often harmed the environment: more cars meant more roads, and more yachts meant more marinas. It multiplied the production of waste, not all of it biodegradable. It sometimes seemed to glorify greed and snobbery, especially when it passed some people by. It troubled the young and the thoughtful: their material needs sated, they might be left asking, "So what?" With money more plentiful, it was easier to be spendthrift. With greater prosperity, drug abuse and alcoholism became more common; so, paradoxically, did hooliganism and casual crime. One of the by-products of the affluent society was self-doubt and self-questioning—the kind of critique of "consumer values" that was voiced by student rebels in and around 1968. It left many Europeans unsure of their deeper objectives and, still more, of their role in a bewildering world.

THE REFLUX OF EMPIRE

One major change in the world during the decades that followed World War II was the emergence of more than 50 new sovereign states. Essentially, this was the result of decolonization.

Before World War II the countries of western Europe had ruled, controlled, or powerfully influenced vast tracts of territory overseas. The main exceptions were Spain, which had long since lost its empire, and

Germany, whose colonies had been confiscated after World War I. Otherwise, Belgium, Britain, France, Italy, the Netherlands, and Portugal remained imperial powers, holding direct or indirect sway over most of Southeast Asia, parts of the West Indies, nearly all of Africa, and much of the Middle East.

Gradually, what had once been colonies, protectorates, or client states won their independence. Some 800 million people were now responsible for their own affairs. Few were richer or more secure. Many retained links with Europe—linguistic, cultural, economic, or commercial; many depended on European investment and aid. But they were free of their colonial masters. Painfully, and sometimes violently, the old order had been superseded, and new relationships had to be built.

The Italian colonies in North and East Africa, like the Japanese empire in East Asia, were dismantled fairly quickly. Independence likewise came early to various Middle Eastern countries, although for many years European influence there continued. Egypt had become formally independent in 1922, Iraq in 1932, and Lebanon and Syria in 1941. Iran's independence was guaranteed by Britain and the U.S.S.R. in 1942. The year 1946 saw Jordan's independence, and 1948 the proclamation of Israel. Historical ties (including the memory of Hitler's Holocaust), strategic pressures, and the need for Middle Eastern oil kept Europe deeply involved in the area long after most of its countries' formal independence had become much more real. The Suez expedition of 1956 actually brought down a British government; oil price rises in the 1970s caused a European recession; and Saddam Hussein's invasion of Kuwait in 1990 for a time seemed to threaten the risk of world war.

British and Dutch decolonization in Asia began in 1947 with the independence of India and the creation of Pakistan. Burma and Ceylon followed in 1948 and the Dutch East Indies in 1949. Malaya's independence was delayed until 1957 by a communist campaign of terror, quelled by both a sophisticated antiguerrilla campaign and a serious effort to win what the British General Sir Gerald Templer called "the hearts and minds of the Malayan people."

French decolonization proved more troublesome. France had given the name "Indo-China" to a million square miles in Southeast Asia, an area nearly 10 times the size of the mother country, which it had colonized in the 19th century—a union of settlements and dependencies in Tonkin, Annam, Laos, Cambodia, and Cochinchina around Saigon. As early as 1925, the Vietnam Revolutionary Party had been founded to fight for the unity and independence of Tonkin, Annam, and Cochinchina. In 1945 it proclaimed a democratic republic and fought the French for eight years. Following the French defeat at Dien Bien Phu in 1954, Vietnam became independent and was partitioned between Hanoi and Saigon. When communist North Vietnam began threatening and attacking the South, the United States was drawn into 10 years of unsuccessful and divisive hostilities, at a heavy cost in human life and political credibility.

France faced similar problems in North Africa. Morocco and Tunisia obtained independence in 1956, but Algeria, legally part of the French republic, aroused far fiercer passions and led to another eight-year war, from 1954 to 1962. Whereas Dien Bien Phu had brought down a French government, the Algerian War caused the downfall of the French Fourth Republic and the accession to power of de Gaulle, who had been in retirement (his second) since 1951. French settlers in Algeria cheered him when he told them: "I have understood you." Only later did they realize that his understanding embraced the need to grant Algeria independence and to crush attempted coups on the part of the settlers' right wing.

In sub-Saharan Africa, what Harold Macmillan called "the wind of change" blew less stormily. There were violent incidents and atrocities, as in the former Belgian Congo, and there were tribal and civil wars. Some white settlers hotly resisted decolonization, as in Rhodesia and South Africa. But by the early 1990s only South Africa maintained white supremacy, and even there the apartheid system was dismantled by 1994. Europeans were aghast at Africa's recurrent famines and concerned at the persistence of apartheid. Yet no aspect of Africa's development seemed likely to affect Europe as deeply as Indochina and Algeria had affected France.

One feature of the postcolonial period, however, was the reflux into Europe of emigrants from the former colonies. Some, civil servants and business people, had little difficulty in settling themselves. Others faced racism. In Britain the first such immigrant groups, from the West Indies, were broadly welcomed. But between 1950 and 1957 Britain's immigrant population doubled, to 200,000, and the busy diligence of Indian and Pakistani shopkeepers, though welcomed by many, also aroused envy and hostility, as it had in Uganda, whence some of them had fled. In France, too, there was racial hostility, directed more often against North Africans than against black immigrants. Neither France nor Britain seemed to have studied the careful preparations that the Netherlands had made to meet similar problems with immigrants from East Asia.

In eastern Europe there was also pressure for independence from quasi-colonial rule. Signs of unrest had begun in Poland, where in June and July 1956 strikes and riots in Poznań had ended with the deaths of 53 workers. In October of that year in Hungary, there was a full-scale revolt, finally quelled on November 4 by Soviet

A crowd gathers around the Berlin Wall in November 1989 after part of it was torn down. The breaching of the wall symbolized a renewal of communication between the eastern and western areas of the city and the eventual reunification of Germany. The Washington Post/Getty Images

tanks. A similar fate ended the "Prague Spring" of 1968 in Czechoslovakia. For a long time, it seemed as if eastern Europe would never be free.

Yet there too the winds of change were blowing. The accession to power of Mikhail S. Gorbachev in 1985 marked a real turning point in the U.S.S.R.: *glasnost* ("openness") replaced compulsive secrecy, and attempts at *perestroika* ("restructuring") sought to replace with efficiency the dead hand of state control. Already in Poland the workers' leader Lech Wałęsa had rallied supporters round the union banner of Solidarity; in Poland and elsewhere, as the 1980s ended, a new era began. Victims were rehabilitated; oppressive regimes were overthrown; dictators were executed; and free elections were held. For many, the most moving moment was on the night of Nov. 9–10, 1989, when the Berlin Wall was breached. Erected by the East German authorities in 1961 to prevent their citizens from fleeing to the West, the Wall was a concrete symbol of the division of Berlin, of Germany, and of Europe. Less than a year later, on Oct. 3, 1990, Germany and Berlin were both formally reunited. How long would it be before Europe was reunited too?

EVER CLOSER UNION?

Discussed by philosophers for centuries, actively promoted from the 1920s onward by Count Richard Coudenhove-Kalergi's Pan-European Movement, and officially proposed in 1929 by Aristide Briand on behalf of France, the idea of uniting Europe was revived again as World War II approached. In Britain a small private group that called itself Federal Union—in close touch with others at the Royal Institute of International Affairs (Chatham House)—began to campaign for unity in Europe as a last frail hope of preventing war. Some of the papers produced by its distinguished supporters, including work by Lord Lothian and Lionel Robbins, found their way to another group of activists in the Italian Resistance, led by, among others, Altiero Spinelli. One of the most stubborn of Mussolini's political prisoners, he was freed in 1943 from confinement on an island off the coast between Rome and Naples. Admiring what he called "the clean, precise thinking of the English federalists," he echoed it in the declaration he drafted for a secret grouping of Resistance leaders from eight other countries, including Germany. Britain thus contributed to Continental developments that British governments shunned for many years.

Support for European unity came from the right as well as the left, from liberals as well as *dirigistes*, from clerics as well as anticlericals, from "Atlanticists" as well as those who saw Europe as a "Third Force" between East and West. It even received official support, overt as well as implicit.

In 1939 the British Labour Party leader Clement Attlee declared: "Europe must federate or perish." In 1940, prompted by Jean Monnet, Churchill's government, in agreement with General de Gaulle, proposed a political union between Britain and France. In 1943 Churchill called for a Council of Europe after the war, and de Gaulle's colleague René Mayer suggested an economic federation. In 1944 the exiled governments of Belgium, the Netherlands, and Luxembourg signed the Benelux Convention for a future customs union. Pope Pius XII, meanwhile, had envisaged a close union of European states.

Individual supporters of European unity included not only statesmen such as Paul-Henri Spaak from Belgium, Alcide De Gasperi from Italy, Robert Schuman from France, Johan Willem Beyen from the Netherlands, Konrad Adenauer from Germany, and Joseph Bech from Luxembourg but also such well-known writers as Albert Camus, Raymond Aron, George Orwell, Denis de Rougemont, and Ignazio Silone. All urged, and many helped to organize, what Winston Churchill called in 1946 "a kind of United States of Europe."

In 1948 a number of activist organizations, coordinated by Joseph Retinger, former assistant to the late General Władysław Sikorski, head of the wartime Polish government-in-exile in London, staged a full-scale Congress of Europe in The Hague. Attended by 750 statesmen from throughout western Europe, including Spaak, De Gasperi, Churchill, Schuman, Adenauer, and a young French Resistance worker named François Mitterrand, it called for political and economic union, a European Assembly, and a European Court of Human Rights.

Some governments responded sympathetically. The postwar constitutions of France, West Germany, and Italy all envisaged limiting national sovereignty: the German text specifically looked forward to a united Europe. The British, however, were skeptical, and when in response to proposals by the French foreign minister Georges Bidault (who had attended The Hague Congress) the governments took action, it was of limited scope. In May 1949 they set up the Council of Europe, consisting of a Committee of Ministers and a Consultative Assembly.

To the activists, it was something, but it was not enough. The Council of Europe's main achievement, apart from useful studies and discussions, was to produce the European Convention for the Protection of Human Rights (1950), effectively backed by a court and a commission. But the Consultative Assembly was just that: it had no power, and the Committee of Ministers had a veto.

The initiative to go further came from Monnet. His opportunity came when France was at loggerheads with Britain and the United States, both of which sought to remove the postwar restraints preventing German heavy industry from making its full contribution to the prosperity of the West. Monnet proposed to sidestep the dilemma by pooling coal and steel production in western Europe, including West Germany's, under common institutions to replace with a light and shared rein the heavy control that the International Ruhr Authority had imposed on West Germany alone.

This was the essence of what became the Schuman Plan in 1950 when Robert Schuman, by then the French foreign minister, accepted it after Georges Bidault, the prime minister, had neglected to take it up. Its end product, initially embracing only six nations, was the formation of the European Coal and Steel Community, which began work in 1952.

Monnet and Schuman saw this as only a first step on the way to a European federation. Monnet followed it by proposing to René Pleven a similar solution to the problem of German rearmament: a European Defense Community. When that eventually failed, he proposed to Spaak and Beyen what became by 1957–58, via the Treaties of Rome, the European Economic Community (EEC) and the European Atomic Energy Community (Euratom), a similar organization for the peaceful use of nuclear energy. The three institutions were ultimately merged to become the European Communities (EC) in 1967. With a Council of Ministers to make essential decisions (if need be by majority vote), a Commission to propose policy, and a European Parliament and Court of Justice to exert, respectively, legislative and judicial control, the EC had the embryo of a federal constitution, limited to economic and social affairs.

It also had the potential for crises, growth, and enlargement. Its first major crisis, indeed, concerned enlargement, when President de Gaulle vetoed the first British application to join, in 1963. The second crisis, two years later, was also provoked by de Gaulle, who objected to the extension of majority voting.

Weathering both crises, the EC proceeded to broaden its scope and to expand beyond the organization's original six members—France, West Germany, Italy, Belgium, Luxembourg, and the Netherlands. First came Britain, Ireland, and Denmark (1973), followed by Greece (1981) and then Spain and Portugal (1986). The Single European Act, promulgated July 1, 1987, built upon ongoing efforts at further social and economic cohesion and established a timetable for the completion of a common market. The Maastricht Treaty (Treaty on European Union), signed

Members of the European Parliament vote on a proposed EU constitution in 2005. Lacking support from voters in France and the Netherlands, the constitution failed and was eventually replaced by the Lisbon Treaty in 2009. Gerard Cerles/AFP/Getty Images

on Feb. 7, 1992, created the European Union (EU), comprising three main components: a common foreign and security policy, an enhanced cooperation in domestic affairs, and the EC, renamed the European Community, which became the anchor of the EU with broader authority. Moreover, the treaty established EU citizenship, which

Lisbon Treaty

The Lisbon Treaty is an international agreement that amended the Maastricht Treaty, Treaties of Rome, and other documents to simplify and streamline the institutions that govern the European Union. Proposed in 2007, the Lisbon Treaty was ratified by most member states in 2008, but a referendum in Ireland—the only country that put the Lisbon agreement to a public vote—rejected it on June 12, 2008, putting in jeopardy the entire treaty. More than a year later, on Oct. 2, 2009, Ireland held a second referendum, which passed. Poland's government also had expressed reservations, but it ratified the treaty a week after the Irish vote, after securing opt-outs from EU policy on some social issues, such as abortion. The Czech Republic was the last remaining holdout: though its Parliament had ratified the treaty, the country's president, Václav Klaus, withheld his signature. Finally, after the Czech courts ruled that the treaty did not violate the country's constitution, Klaus signed it on Nov. 3, 2009. The Lisbon Treaty, thus ratified by all 27 member states, entered into force on Dec. 1, 2009.

While it was not explicitly called a European constitution, the treaty addressed a number of issues that had been central to the 2004 EU draft constitution, an initiative that was scuttled after voters in France and the Netherlands rejected it in 2005. Under the amendments of the Lisbon Treaty, the European Community—which had provided the economic framework upon which the EU was built—disappeared, and its powers and structure were incorporated into the EU. Moreover, the office of a permanent EU president was created, with the president chosen by the leaders of the member countries from a pool of candidates that they had selected. The leader holding this two-and-a-half-year post, officially called the president of the European Council, would provide a "face" for the EU in matters of Union policy. (The rotating EU presidency, whereby each member country assumes a leadership role for a period of six months, was retained, although its mandate would be narrowed.) Another new position, that of high representative for foreign affairs and security policy, gathered the EU's two foreign affairs portfolios into a single office, with the goal of creating a more robust and unified European foreign policy. The power of the European Parliament also was enhanced and its number of seats revised. Additionally, the Charter of Fundamental Rights, initially proposed at the Council of Nice in 2000, entered into force as part of the Lisbon Treaty. It spelled out a host of civil, political, economic, and social rights guaranteed to all citizens of the EU.

Perhaps the most sweeping changes, though, were to the voting mechanisms that determined EU policy. Within the Council of the European Union—the EU's main decision-making body—the system of qualified majority voting (QMV), previously used only in certain circumstances, was extended to more policy areas, thereby easing the decision-making process. In addition, for most decisions, 55 percent of member states, provided they represented 65 percent of the EU's population, would be able to approve a measure. This "double majority" voting rule, which represents a simplification of the former system of weighted votes, would be phased in over time. Matters of defense, foreign policy, social security, and taxation would still require unanimous approval, however. While QMV and the "double majority" rule were designed to streamline decision making at the highest levels, critics argued that they would reduce the influence of smaller countries at the expense of larger ones. Partly to address this, the Lisbon Treaty introduced the European Citizens' Initiative, a process by which EU citizens could directly petition the European Commission (the EU's main executive body) by gathering one million signatures from a number of member states.

allowed citizens, regardless of nationality, to vote and run for office in elections in the country of their residence both for local office and for the organization's increasingly important legislative body, the European Parliament. Enthusiasm for the EU in the member countries was not universal (it took two referendums for Danish voters to approve their country's involvement, and the referendum on membership was barely approved by the French electorate), but the treaty officially took effect on Nov. 1, 1993. "Convergence criteria" (relating to levels of government spending, inflation, public debt, and exchange-rate stability) were established for participation in a common European currency. Although some countries failed to qualify (Greece) or chose to remain outside the system (Britain, Denmark, and Sweden, the last having joined the EU in 1995 along with Austria and Finland), 11 countries on Jan. 1, 1999, relinquished control over their exchange rates and began a transition to the replacement of their national currencies with a single monetary unit, the euro.

Meanwhile, members of the EU began acting collectively in foreign policy, notably attempting to bring peace to the countries of the former federation of Yugoslavia, which splintered violently, beginning with the secession of Croatia and Slovenia in 1991 and that of Macedonia in 1992. Ethnic civil war was more protracted in Bosnia and Herzegovina (sparking UN intervention), and EU members helped halt the fighting there through participation in the brokering of the Dayton Accords. Acting under the aegis of NATO, a number of EU countries intervened militarily in the conflict in Kosovo (1998–99) between that region's ethnic Albanian majority and Serbian minority and government of the rump Yugoslavia state (comprising Serbia and Montenegro) and again in Afghanistan, where the Taliban regime had provided a home for the radical Islamists responsible for the September 11 attacks on the United States in 2001. Terrorist bombings by Islamist radicals also struck Europe, in Madrid in March 2004 and in London in July 2005.

In 2004 the EU admitted 10 more countries: the Czech Republic and Slovakia (independent states formed by the dissolution of Czechoslovakia in 1992), as well as Cyprus, Estonia, Hungary, Latvia, Lithuania, Malta, Poland, and Slovenia. Bulgaria and Romania joined in 2007. Other than Cyprus and Malta, the 21st-century additions were all former members of the communist bloc. To the consternation of Russia, many of them also joined NATO. In

2008 Russia showed its support for Serbia (a solitary country after the split in 2006 of Serbia and Montenegro, the renamed loose successor state to Yugoslavia), when Kosovo declared its independence despite Serbian opposition. Russia's relations with the EU and NATO, particularly those organizations' former communist members, were sometimes tense, as when Russia objected strenuously to U.S. plans to deploy a missile-defense radar system in the Czech Republic and Poland.

Efforts begun in 2002 to draft a constitution for the enlarged EU led to the signing of a document in 2004 that failed to be ratified by French and Dutch voters in 2005. A reform version of the failed constitution, stewarded by Germany, resulted in the Lisbon Treaty of December 2007; however, it too was scuttled, at least temporarily, when Irish voters rejected it in 2008. In October 2009 Ireland approved the treaty in a second referendum, and Poland completed its ratification process as well. That November the Czech Republic became the final country to ratify the treaty, which entered into force on Dec. 1, 2009.

The EC was founded in response to a checkered half-century of European history, when some of the world's most civilized countries had plumbed depths of savagery, folly, tyranny, and genocide that in a work of science fiction would be hard to believe. The EC's most obvious purpose had been to reconcile former enemies and prevent war. Its second aim was to avoid the economic errors Europeans had made in the 1930s, when, instead of collaborating on a global recovery policy in response to the Great Depression, they worsened the crisis through economic nationalism that was the breeding ground for dictatorship. Moreover, Europe's individual countries, once great powers, were dwarfed numerically, politically, and militarily by the United States and the Soviet Union (until its dissolution in 1991–92) and economically by the

United States and Japan. By the early 21st century the gigantic countries of India and China had also become economic rivals for the European Union and for a Europe that increasingly saw greater cohesiveness as the path not only to holding its own vis-à-vis political and economic superpowers but also to maximizing its power to meet its wider responsibilities in the world.

CONCLUSION

The modern era of European history encompasses the 19th and 20th centuries and extends into the 21st. The first portion of this era is bounded by two great events. The French Revolution broke out in 1789, and its effects reverberated throughout much of Europe for many decades. World War I began in 1914; its inception resulted from many trends in European society, culture, and diplomacy during the late 19th century. In between these boundaries—the one opening a new set of trends, the other bringing long-standing tensions to a head—much of modern Europe was defined.

Europe during this 125-year span was both united and deeply divided. Industrialization sparked dramatic economic and social changes in virtually every country. A number of cultural currents, including new literary and artistic styles and the spread of science, ran through the entire continent. Meanwhile, European states were increasingly locked in diplomatic interaction, culminating in continentwide alliance systems after 1871. Indeed, the 1800s were a century of growing nationalism, in which individual states jealously protected their identities and indeed established more rigorous border controls than ever before.

The 20th century ushered in a period of spectacular change. Continued industrialization and remarkable advances in technology accompanied the development of a mass society and new forms of recreation. World War I, however, brought widespread disillusionment. The war not only cost millions of European lives; it also exacerbated nationalism and ideological extremism. Its unsatisfactory resolution in 1918 contributed to the outbreak in 1939 of World War II, the largest and bloodiest conflict in world history.

With two world wars in the first half of the 20th century, Europe had come close to destroying itself. Consequently, European statesmen began to seek ways of uniting Europe peacefully, on a basis of equality instead of domination by one or more great powers. European unity, they believed, would prevent further wars in Europe; it also would allow Europe to match the political and economic influence of the world's new superpowers, the United States and the Soviet Union.

Unity in Europe is an ancient ideal. The Roman Empire, the medieval empire of Charlemagne, and the Holy Roman Empire were early versions of a united Europe. Later, Napoleon Bonaparte and Adolf Hitler tried to unite Europe by conquest. The union created in the second half of the 20th century, however, was based neither on military might nor on the national interests of individual states. Rather, the European Communities and their successor, the European Union, were based on common rules and institutions that promoted the shared interests of Europe. By the early 21st century, the European Union had expanded beyond western Europe to embrace a number of countries in central and eastern Europe. Although critics of the European Union continued to question its scope, its supporters remained convinced that Europeans—a mosaic of different peoples with a multiplicity of languages—have more in common than divides them, especially in the modern world.

Glossary

abeyance Temporary inactivity; suspension.

animus Basic attitude or disposition; also, a usually prejudiced and often spiteful or malevolent ill will.

assiduous Marked by careful unremitting attention or persistent application.

carapace A protective, decorative, or disguising shell.

charlatanry A showy or pretentious demonstration of knowledge or ability that one does not actually have.

conciliation The act of making compatible; appeasement.

conduce To lead or tend to a particular and often desirable result; contribute.

dialectic Characterized by discussion and reasoning by dialogue as a method of intellectual investigation.

fountainhead Principal source; origin.

fulsome Characterized by abundance; copious.

intendant An administrative official, especially under the French, Spanish, or Portuguese monarchies.

inveigh To protest or complain bitterly or vehemently.

itinerant Travelling from place to place.

joint-stock venture A forerunner of the modern corporation in which money was raised by selling shares to investors, who became partners in the venture.

journeyman A worker who has learned a trade and works for another person usually by the day.

kulak Wealthy or prosperous landed peasant in Russia.

leitmotiv A melodic idea associated with a character or an important dramatic element.

manorialism Political, economic, and social system, dating from the medieval period, by which peasants were tied to their land and their lord through serfdom.

maudlin Weakly and effusively sentimental.
moribund Being in a state of inactivity or obsolescence.
necromancy Communication with the dead, usually to obtain insight into the future or to accomplish some otherwise impossible task.
parricide The murder of a parent or close relative.
pedantry The presentation or application of knowledge in a narrow, stodgy, and often ostentatious manner.
platitudinous Having the characteristics of a platitude; banal, trite, or stale in nature.
plenary Fully attended or constituted by all entitled to be present.
plenipotentiary A person and especially a diplomatic agent invested with full power to transact business.
ply To make a practice of rowing or sailing over or on.
positivism A theory that theology and metaphysics are earlier imperfect modes of knowledge and that positive knowledge is based on natural phenomena and their properties and relations as verified by the empirical sciences.
prevaricate To deviate from the truth; equivocate.
putsch A secretly plotted and suddenly executed attempt to overthrow a government.
sedulous Involving or accomplished with careful perseverance.
syndicalism Movement advocating direct action by the working class to abolish the capitalist order, including the state, and to replace it with a social order based on the syndicate, a free association of self-governing producers.
vicissitude A difficulty or hardship attendant on a way of life, a career, or a course of action and usually beyond one's control.
welter A chaotic mass or jumble.

Bibliography

Comprehensive coverage of the first portion of the modern era is offered in Robin W. Winks and Thomas Kaiser, *Europe, 1648–1815: From the Old Regime to the Age of Revolution* (2004); and T.C.W. Blanning (ed.), *The Nineteenth Century: Europe, 1789–1914* (2000). Jeremy D. Popkin, *A Short History of the French Revolution*, 2nd ed. (1998), is a brief overview of the event. Theodore S. Hamerow, *The Birth of a New Europe: State and Society in the Nineteenth Century* (1983), provides an excellent introduction to the period following the French Revolution. A treatment of the Industrial Revolution and related social developments is Lenard R. Berlanstein (ed.), *The Industrial Revolution and Work in Nineteenth-Century Europe* (1992). Other important sociological studies include Bonnie G. Smith, *Changing Lives: Women in European History since 1700* (1989); and Harvey J. Graff (ed.), *Literacy and Social Development in the West* (1981). The historical role of Romanticism is addressed in Nicholas Roe (ed.), *Romanticism: An Oxford Guide* (2005).

Developments in the mid-to-late 19th century are studied in Peter N. Stearns, *1848: The Revolutionary Tide in Europe* (1974); Albert S. Lindemann, *A History of European Socialism* (1983); and Robin W. Winks and Joan Neuberger, *Europe and the Making of Modernity, 1815–1914* (2005). An overview of imperialism can be found in V. G. Kiernan, *European Empires from Conquest to Collapse, 1815–1960* (1982). Arno J. Mayer, *The Persistence of the Old Regime: Europe to the Great War* (1981), interprets internal European diplomatic patterns. Realism in the arts is treated in William W. Stowe, *Balzac, James, and the Realistic Novel* (1983); and Lorenz Eitner, *19th-Century European Painting: David to Cézanne*, rev. ed. (2002).

General historical surveys of Europe after 1914 include Jean-Baptiste Duroselle, *Europe: A History of Its People* (1990; originally published in French, 1990); and H. Stuart Hughes and James Wilkinson, *Contemporary Europe: A History*, 7th ed. (1991). World War I is examined in Spencer Tucker, *The Great War, 1914–1918* (1998). David Clay Large, *Between Two Fires: Europe's Path in the 1930s* (1990); and Eugen Weber, *The Hollow Years* (1994), treat the interwar period. The approach and developments of World War II are summarized in Martin Gilbert, *The Second World War: A Complete History* (1989).

The postwar situation is examined in Derek W. Urwin, *Western Europe Since 1945: A Political History*, 4th ed. (1989); and Walter LaFeber, *America, Russia, and the Cold War, 1945–1992* (1993). T. Iván Berend, *An Economic History of Twentieth-Century Europe: Economic Regimes from Laissez-Faire to Globalization* (2006), offers an economic perspective. The development of European unity is discussed in Desmond Dinan, *Ever Closer Union: An Introduction to European Integration*, 3rd ed. (2005); and John McCormick, *The European Union: Politics and Policies*, 4th ed. (2008).

Index

C

D

E

F

G

H

M

N

O

P

T

U

V

W

Y

Z